The
CANADIAN NATIONAL
RAILWAYS' STORY

GRAND TRUNK WESTERN NO. 56's consist was expanded significantly with thru Chicago-Detroit equipment from No. 20 at Durand. Here 56 whips by Bloomfield Hills with one box express car, one baggage car, two coaches, one parlor car, one more coach and one baggage car carrying the markers for a total of seven cars.

Elmer Treloar

The CANADIAN NATIONAL RAILWAYS' STORY

BY

PATRICK C. DORIN

SUPERIOR PUBLISHING COMPANY, SEATTLE

simultaneously published in Canada by

HANCOCK HOUSE PUBLISHERS
SAANICHTON, BRITISH COLUMBIA

Library of Congress Card Number

Library of Congress Cataloging in Publication Data

Dorin, Patrick C.
The Canadian National Railways' story.

Includes index.
1. Canadian National Railways — History.
2. Railroads — Canada — History. I. Title.
HE2810.C14D67 385'0971 75-23240
ISBN 0-87564-522-4

First Edition

Printed and Bound in The United States of America

DEDICATED TO
ALL OFFICERS AND EMPLOYEES
of
CANADIAN NATIONAL RAILWAY SYSTEM

CONTENTS

INTRODUCTION

A railway as large as Canadian National, and with such a diverse background and history, is in many ways a difficult railway to write about. Individual volumes can be written about not only the principal subsidiaries of today (Grand Trunk Western, Duluth, Winnipeg & Pacific and Central Vermont) but also the original component railways of Canadian National.

Therefore the purpose of this volume was to examine the services provided by the CN System from 1919 to 1975. Indeed this author recognizes that this is no small task, and even that history cannot be contained in a volume this size. Therefore the various types of train service are high lighted both historically from 1919 to 1975 and geographically from Newfoundland to British Columbia. As with *Canadian Pacific Railway*, published by Superior Publishing Company in 1974, this book is not a political or economic history.

In order to accomplish the purpose briefly described above, the author has compartmentized the book into several sections. The first chapter contains a brief description of the development of Canadian National Railways. The next three chapters cover the passenger train services including the suburban districts and the Super Continental. The next three chapters look at the freight and mixed train services plus a closer look at the iron ore and grain traffic.

The next three chapters cover different aspects of CN service including the electric interurban routes, the narrow gauge route in Newfoundland and the biggest most recent railway construction project in North America in recent years, the Great Slave Lake Railway.

Following that comes the important US subsidiaries and finally a brief overview of other CN operations throughout Canada.

Canadian National Railways has been absolutely essential to the economies of Canada and the United States. The Federal Government of Canada recognized this during the period from 1910 to 1923 when CN was slowing being organized. The Government had the wisdom and understanding to realize that without a railway certain territories would never be able to develop. It was a situation where the Government had to take action or possibly let many route miles of railway die that were critically needed.

CN is now over 50 years young. It is obvious that many of the right decisions were made because her efficiency and ability to serve the shipping and traveling public have improved substantially over the years. Indeed it could be said that the last five years from 1970 to 1975 have been among the most exciting of CN's history. The next half of this decade promises to be even more exciting as expanding traffic levels dictate new trackage and train service concepts. The Research and Development Department is playing a key role in these new developments. A second volume needs to be written describing this most exciting era of all on Canadian National Railways.

Many people have offered a great deal of assistance to this writer during the research and writing of *The Canadian National Railways' Story*. Without their kind help and time, sometimes spending long hours going over materials, the book simply could not have been written. The author wishes to gratefully acknowledge the following people for their seemingly never ending ability to give their time and energies to my writing projects:

Mr. Albert P. Salisbury of Superior Publishing Company for his encouragement and work with the layout through to the final publication of the book.

My wife, Karen, who seems to have an unlimited supply of energy to check materials, photographs and all kinds of details.

Mr. Luther Miller of Railway Age for permission to use Railway Age and Railway Age Gazette from 1919 to 1975 as resource materials.

Mr. Jerry Delling who assisted me with printing photographs and has given freely of his time with techniques of photography.

Mr. Chip Rogers for several hours of time going over Grand Trunk Western Railroad materials, and Mr. Roger Gryskiewicz who spent countless hours in the St. Paul, Minnesota library going over historical data for this writer. Photographs came from many sources including Mr. Elmer Treloar, Mr. Jim Scribbins (who also provided substantial historical and geographical data for the book), Mr. Harold K. Vollrath, Mr. Dale Wilson, Mr. William A. Raia, Mr. John H. Kuehl, Mr. Bob Lorenz, Mr. Jack W. Swanberg, Mr. Dick George, Mr. Al Paterson, Mr. Tom Hoff, Mr. Stan F. Styles, Mr. Paul Stringham, Mr. A. Robert Johnson, Mr. Jim Morin, and Mr. Sy Dykhouse.

I am particularly indebted to Mr. Duncan Haimerl of CN's Public Relations Department who spent long hours with me over weekends riding trains, going over materials and answering thousands of questions. Mr. Bob Boden of Photographic Services has now assisted this author with photographs for four different books. Mr. Tom Henry assisted with GO Transit materials. Mr. Jack Skull of the Prairie Region, Mr. H. C. Lear and Mr. Philip Larson on the Duluth, Winnipeg and Pacific Railway, and many, many others with Grand Trunk Western and Central Vermont have given much of their time and energies to *The Canadian National Railways' Story.*

North Branch, Minnesota   Patrick C. Dorin
March 31, 1975

CHAPTER 1

The Development of Canadian National Railways

Canada entered railroading early in its history. A group of Montreal businessmen were granted a charter for the construction of the Champlain and St. Lawrence in 1832. It took four more years before the 14½-mile-long railroad went into operation as a portage or land link in the water route between Montreal and New York. The line connected Laprairie on the St. Lawrence River with St. Jean on the Richelieu River. The railway was the only line in Canada for nearly 10 years.

The second Canadian railway was the Montreal and Lachine, opened in 1847 to replace a stagecoach route around the Lachine Rapids. Both railways were eventually acquired by the Grand Trunk Railway.

The Grand Trunk, which was chartered in 1852, eventually became a major component in the formation of Canadian National. At about the same time, the provincial governments of Nova Scotia, New Brunswick and Prince Edward Island went into the railway construction business. As they proved unable to make a go of them, the Dominion Government took over the segmented lines and built the Intercolonial Railway. The route connected the Grand Trunk at Riviere-du-Loup with the eastern seaboard, and the first step toward what would finally become a unified Canadian National Railway was completed.

The Intercolonial was completed in 1876, having acquired the Prince Edward Island Railway in 1873. The term "Canadian Government Railways" was gradually adopted for the Intercolonial and other government-owned lines during the subsequent decades.

From this point in time, the events that led to the formation of Canadian National have deep financial roots. The Grand Trunk Railway, without sufficient funds for expansion, entered into an agreement with the Federal Government for a railroad construction project that would link the east and the west. The Grand Trunk agreed to build a line from Winnipeg to Prince Rupert, British Columbia. This section of railway was called the Grand Trunk Pacific Railway and was completed in April, 1914.

The other section of railway was to be built by the Canadian Government from Winnipeg to Moncton. This line was to be known as the National Transcontinental and leased by the Grand Trunk Pacific upon completion. However due to financial difficulties, the Grand Trunk Pacific could not carry out its part of the agreement. The line had to be taken over, for operation, by the Canadian Government Railways in May, 1915. One month later, it opened for traffic throughout.

The Grand Trunk, along with the Grand Trunk Pacific, had now become a giant among railways with a 7,500 mile system, steamships in intercoastal trade on the Pacific Ocean, large grain elevators on tidewater and a number of fine hotels.

As the Canadian Government Railways was expanding, the Canadian Northern grew from a few hundred miles in 1901 to over 9,000 miles in 1915. The system extended from Montreal to Vancouver, but she grew too fast without concern for solid financial footing. At the same time, Canada was having financial difficulties and two of the major railway systems were on the verge of failure.

World War I drained the resources of the railways. As they were vitally needed by the nation, the Canadian Government took a number of steps to consolidate the financially-troubled railways.

A Royal Commission studied the problem and, upon its recommendations, an act of Parliament provided for the taking over of the Canadian Northern by the federal government. The year was 1917.

At that time, the Canadian Government Railways comprised a number of railways of which the two most important components were the Intercolonial between Montreal and Halifax, Sydney, Charlottetown and Saint John; and the National Transcontinental from Moncton to Winnipeg with a grand total mileage of 4,105. The next step, taken by the government in 1918, was to entrust these lines to the directors of the Canadian Northern. In June, 1919 the Canadian National Railway Company was incorporated to operate the Canadian Northern, Canadian Government Railways and all railways that were or were to become the prop-

CANADIAN NORTHERN BEGAN as a modest carrier between the Great Lakes and the West, but rapid expansion brought its financial house tumbling down. The CN initials were easily applicable to the new Canadian National name.

Canadian National

erty of the Dominion of Canada. (The reader should take notice that 1918 is the year that the name Canadian National Railways was authorized.)

However the Canadian National as we know it today was still five years off, but in the meantime it would grow partially. Financial disaster had struck the Grand Trunk Pacific and in February, 1920 that entire line was added to the Canadian National. Following prolonged negotiations the Grand Trunk was amalgamated with CN in January, 1923. This step was a little more complicated because the Grand Trunk operated railways in the United States, including the Central Vermont. Therefore for technical and legal reasons, all Grand Trunk lines west of the Detroit and St. Clair rivers were renamed Grand Trunk Western Railroad. Grand Trunk lines in New England retained the name Grand Trunk Railway while the Central Vermont Railway continued to maintain the separate identity it had since coming under Grand Trunk Railway control.

The same procedure was used with the Duluth, Winnipeg & Pacific, which retains its name to this day.

Over the years, Canadian National absorbed a number of small railroads, but the last major addition was the 705-mile narrow gauge Newfoundland Railway in 1949. The most recent acquisition, early this year (1975) was the 35-mile Canada and Gulf Terminal Railway linking Mont Joli and Matane, two Quebec municipalities located on the south shore of the St. Lawrence River.

It is recognized by this author that these few short paragraphs do not do justice to the history of the formation of the Canadian National Railway system. However, to spend more than a few moments with this early history would subtract space in this book from the operating and geographical study of Canadian National from its formation in 1919 through 1975. The next fifteen chapters are devoted to the 56-year period of one of the world's largest and best known railways.

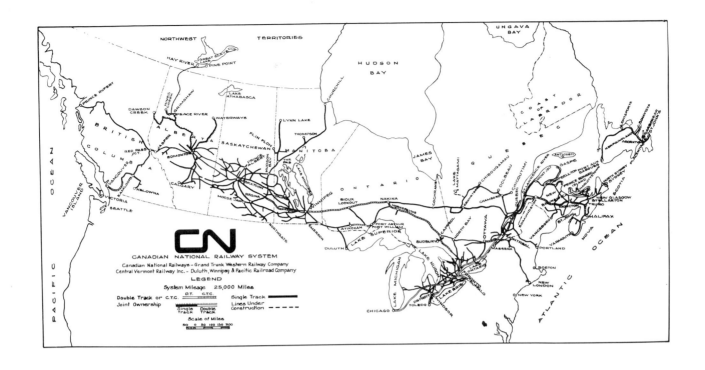

THE GRAND TRUNK RAILWAY at the time of amalgamation was one of Canada's largest railways, and its lines served several states in the USA. This photo was taken in 1912 at Lewiston, Maine.

Harold K. Vollrath Collection

GRAND TRUNK PACIFIC Railway passenger train pauses at Pacific, British Columbia with a 4-4-0 steam locomotive, which seems to be rather light for the heavy passenger train consist. Note the horizontal bars on the pilot of the 111 and the size of the crowd on the depot platform. The photo was taken between 1915 and 1920.

Canadian National Railways

THE INTERCOLONIAL RAILWAY's Ocean Limited scoots along behind a Ten Wheeler, No. 69, which was built in 1901. 69 was later renumbered 615 for the Canadian Government Railways, and carried the number 1522 for Canadian National. The Ocean Limited was an all-sleeping car train for a good deal of its career.

Canadian National Railways

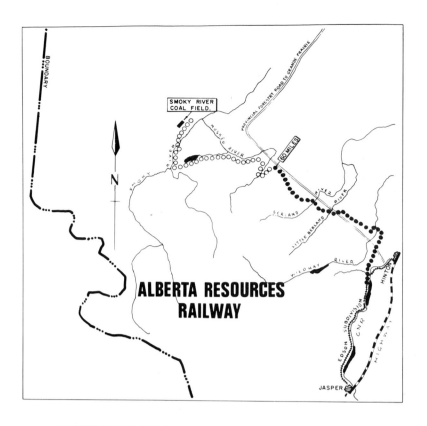

AS WE MOVE through the 1970's, Canadian National is still involved with new railway trackage, such as the new Alberta Resources Railway (which CN will operate) being built to tap new energy resources.

ALTHOUGH MOST CANADIAN National Railway System trackage in the United States is operated by the Duluth, Winnipeg & Pacific; Central Vermont, Grand Trunk and Grand Trunk Western Railways, there is some CN trackage in the states of New York and Minnesota. Warroad, Minnesota is located on CN's main line between Thunder Bay, Ontario and Winnipeg, Manitoba.

Jim Morin

CHAPTER 2

Passenger Train Service

Our story of Canadian National passenger trains opens in the 1920's during and shortly after the amalgamation of the Grand Trunk Railway System with Canadian National Railways. Service was offered over virtually every mile of the railway, with the exception of a few branch lines such as the short lived route from Fort William, Ontario (now Thunder Bay) to Gunflint Iron Range near the Minnesota border. At the time there were four passenger trains that could be considered fleet leaders. The Continental Limited between Montreal and Vancouver led the fleet. This .was followed by the National between Toronto and Winnipeg, the International Limited between Montreal and Chicago and the Ocean Limited between Montreal and Halifax. All of these trains offered observation cars, sleepers, coach service as well as dining and lounge car service. Of the four trains listed above, only the "Ocean" remains in 1975.

Throughout the 1920's most of the main line trains were equipped with steel cars, but many secondary and branch lines operated with wooden passenger equipment. The mid-1920's also saw the beginning of the erosion of passenger patronage to the automobile. The next half century from 1925 to 1975 has witnessed a complete change in passenger service, and we might add that despite the fact that over 85% of the intercity passenger traffic is by private auto, the Canadian National has maintained a positive attitude. During that time CN has placed a great number of innovations into operation, and has maintained a high quality of service even though there has been a reduction in the number of trains operated since 1925. In many cases service is actually superior to that of 50 years ago, but before we get too far head of ourselves let's take a look at the many innovations in CN passenger service.

The automobile first hit the light traffic lines the hardest. Consequently in late 1925 and early 1926, Canadian National placed in operation an order of 9 diesel electric cars constructed at CN's Point St. Charles shops in Montreal. Seven cars were single units with a length of 60 feet and a passenger capacity of 57 people. The other two were articulated cars 102 feet long and a seating capacity of 126 passengers. It was the light traffic lines that led the road to consider the possibilities of self-propelled passenger equipment which offered the advantages of a reduction in the size of train crews, lower maintenance expenses and greater availability than could be obtained from steam locomotives at that time. What is really interesting is the fact that CN chose a diesel engine for the source of motive power instead of gasoline engines, which were very much in use at that time for such equipment. One of the factors considered in making this decision was the cost of fuel. In 1926 the cost of gasoline to Canadian National was 22¢ per imperial gallon, while the cost of diesel fuel oil was but 12¢. Had gasoline engines of equal power been used, the June 4, 1927 issue of Railway Age reported that it would have cost $78,000 more for the total operation in 1926. RA further reported that the nine cars produced a total revenue of $337,041.45 during 1926. The operating costs were $127,421.73 with a net operating revenue of $209,619.72.

Canadian National also conducted a study of the trains as compared to steam service. The route selected was between Edmonton and Saskatoon. The operating cost of steam was $1.01 per mile while the diesel cars operated for 23¢ per train mile.

Initially the articulated units were assigned to the Guelph, Ontario—Palmerston and the Palmerston, Ontario and Kincardine runs. The other seven cars went into service on the Edmonton and Saskatoon route (2 cars), Quebec City and Richmond, Oxford Junction, N.S. and Truro, Sackville, N.B., Tignish and Charlottetown, Prince Edward Island, Montreal and Waterloo, Quebec, and Ottawa, Ontario and Pembroke. The results were so successful that it lead to the development of the first road diesel built for Canadian National,

IT WAS A long ride from Brandon to Brandon North by bicycle for Jim Scribbins, much of it uphill out of the Assiniboine valley, but the ultimate result was well worthwhile as Mountain No. 6051 moved away from the depot under what is unquestionably the largest smoke plume ever photographed by that rail author/photographer. Moreover, it was, unlike many steam excursions, completely unplanned. The train is the fleet leader, the Montreal section of the Continental Limited and the date is May 29, 1948.

No. 9000, built in 1928. Canadian National was, and still is, a pioneer in motive power development.

The year 1928 is also noted for a new service on day trains which made frequent stops. During that time, CN operated many day trains that did not include dining or parlor car service. Most of the passengers on many of these trains did not travel long distances. It was discovered by trainmen and the Passenger Traffic Department that some of these passengers desired parlor car service, and still others preferred to dine on the train rather than wait until their destination was reached.

The answer for accommodating these passengers was the combination cafe-parlor car already in operation on many longer distance day trains. Thus an order was placed with Canadian Car & Foundry Company for five new cars. The new equipment was divided into two sections with a 15 seat parlor section and table seating for 18 in the dining room. The parlor and dining sections were separated by a smoking room.

The parlor section contained comfortable chairs upholstered in blue leather while the carpeting was a combination blue and sand color.

Movable foot rests were covered with a material similar to the carpeting.

The smoking room contained a 6 foot, 11 inch long sofa plus a washbowl with a mirror over it. The windows were fitted with blue tone pantasote curtains.

The dining room contained six mahogany tables, three of which seated four persons each while the other three were designed for two. The table tops and buffet cupboards were covered with Monel metal, with the carpeting similar to the parlor room. All of the metal trim was of antique silver. The foyer (between the dining room and the kitchen) contained the fruit refrigerator and a soiled linen locker with a self-closing door.

The pantry and kitchen were compact but well equipped. This area contained a cracked ice container, water filter container, two ice wells, a sink, and a cup and plate warmer. The kitchen section contained a coal range and charcoal broiler and a steam table. The kitchen was also equipped with a Bohn vitreous refrigerator that was iced from the roof. It was quite a job climbing a ladder while carrying a cake of ice to be deposited through the roof for the refrigerator.

TRAIN NO. 1, the Montreal section of the Continental, rounds the curve from Transcona heading for the Winnipeg depot, and at the same time blasts up grade trying to arrive on the advertised 9:30 AM. It is April, 1952, and the 14 car train is more than enough tonnage for the 6024, a type U-1-b Mountain.

Photo by George Harris, Collection of Stan F. Styles

The cafe-parlor cars were assigned to various runs out of Toronto, Montreal, Quebec City and Ottawa.

In 1930 Canadian National made the decision to modernize the International Limited between Montreal and Chicago, and the Confederation between Toronto and Vancouver. Altogether five dining cars, 12 lounge cars and 12 sleeping cars were constructed. The 29 cars contained a number of interesting innovations in design, interior finishes and facilities. For example vestibules were eliminated in the dining cars and the extra floor space utilized for other facilities. The new sleepers for the Confederation were designed to give the passenger a choice of upper and lower berths, drawing rooms and single or double bedrooms. The lounge cars for the International Limited included a barber shop, shower bath with facilities for exercising, radio and full time telephone service.

The interiors of the dining cars were finished in walnut veneer from a tree which, according to the October 25, 1930 issue of Railway Age, was green in 1264. This tree stood for nearly seven centuries near the Manor House of Cuxham now part of Oxford University in England. The wood was highly figured and had a beautiful natural grain, and it is interesting to note that the wood was not stained or varnished. It was simply rubbed and polished to a smooth finish. The side panels were of Ancona walnut with border inlays of Coramandel

16

drawing room, one chambrette and three compartments. The interior finish was mahogany with an 18th Century dark finish. The interior decor included maple leaves in autumn tints located on the corners of the berth fronts. The upholstery was blue and grey friezette with blue and sand carpeting harmonizing with the upholstery. The cars were named after prominent Canadian ports, such as Port Alfred, Port Bolster, etc.

The Depression began to strike with fury by 1931. CN began to find itself in a real bind as steps had to be taken to reduce expenses and yet maintain a high standard of service. Studies by the operating and traffic departments revealed some interesting points. It turned out that by increasing the over the road speeds that the company gained an increase in operating efficiency and several other benefits such as, the meeting of highway bus competition, the elimination of certain station stops and delays as a result of the close check up made of the train service when higher speed is contemplated, thereby creating conditions that extended locomotive runs with the additional benefits of decreased fuel consumption (train speeds were more consistent) and a greater monthly mileage per locomotive. This was and is an interesting philosophy in view of the fact that nearly all other North American railroads elected to slow down service to gain economies and greater efficiency.

Another problem that CN tried to solve during the Depression was the dining car financial losses and food waste. An accounting system was set up that monitored the amount of food loaded on dining cars and the gross revenues earned on a given run. The result of this system, and also of a marketing study conducted among passengers, brought about the discontinuance of table d'hote service during the Depression. The study indicated that passengers favored a la carte service, which allowed passengers to order food in any combination they desired. Consequently they could order only food that they liked, and the result was less food thrown out at cleaning time at the end of a run.

Canadian National did not sit back and be content with the new dining car system. From this point they instituted several schemes to get the coach passenger to patronize the dining cars more freely. To accomplish this, CN offered reduced portions from the regular menu (food portions being a little less than two-thirds of the regular portion) and reduced prices. Printed brochures were distributed through the coaches listing menus at the reduced portion prices and showing what could be

from Madagascar for contrast. English grey harewood and amboyna burl was also used in the decoration of the five dining cars. The dining room had a seating capacity of 36 passengers.

The 12 lounge cars contained a vestibule on one end and a solarium with Vita glass windows on the opposite end. The lounge room was finished in maple veneer and elaborately furnished with tables, desks, over-stuffed chairs and davenports. The seats, chairs and davenports were covered with striped blue and grey English hair cloth. The equipment also contained a soda foundation, buffet, barber shop and a bathroom. The latter contained a tiled shower, exerciser and Vibratone.

The sleeping cars were designed primarily for the Confederation, but were operated on other runs as well. Each car contained six sections, one

17

TRAIN NO. 3, the Toronto section of the Continental Limited, eases out of the little frame Brandon North Station, 129 miles from the Manitoba metropolis of Winnipeg. 4-8-2 No. 6050 is doing the honors on this May 29, 1948.

Jim Scribbins

purchased at a fixed price. The result was an increase in dining car patronage for both coach and sleeping car passengers.

Another innovation created during the Depression was the shipment of l.c.l. (less than carload lots) freight on passenger trains. This was accomplished through the purchase of 50 forty foot, forty ton box-baggage cars (sometimes known as box-express cars) that were painted the CN green passenger car color and equipped with passenger type of draft gears, steam heat lines and air signal line. They were lettered similar to CN freight equipment.

About the same time the 50 box-baggage cars were purchased (1938-1939), CN also ordered five mail-baggage cars and ten full baggage cars. These were ordered to replace wooden equipment and also to handle increases in mail and express traffic as the Depression slowly came to a close. The mail cars were also equipped with a water cooler, gas plate, an electric fan over the sorting table and a separate room for a toilet and wash stand. The baggage compartment of the cars contained a hot water heater, coal box, cook stove, desk and waybill case. When this equipment was constructed it contained more conveniences for the baggage and mail crews than could be found on any other equipment. The equipment set a standard for future mail and express cars.

From 1939 Canadian National found itself in the war effort, and every piece of equipment went into service. There were literally no spares. CN carried a total of 144,676,000 passengers from 1939 through 1945. This included 4,381,320 troops requiring 6540 special trains and more than 40 million men and women employed in the war industry. It staggers the imagination that such a job of transportation could have been carried out and completed, but yet it was and the job was done well.

It would be most difficult to answer the question of how CN actually accomplished this task, but it would be well to take a look at a couple of examples—two of the more cheerful ones of troops coming home to their loved ones rather than leaving for the European or Pacific war fronts. In October, 1945, CN handled 20,000 homecoming troops out of Halifax in one week. The Queen Elizabeth docked with 12,000 troops and a train load of civilians. They left Halifax in 27 passenger extras, one every hour until the port was cleared, and this was done with a downpour of rain that last 18 hours. About the same time the Ile de France sailed into Halifax with enough troops and civilians for 23 passenger specials. As soon as the trains were emptied they were turned back to the east coast for still more homecoming people. The war had made unprecedented demands on the resources of the railway, but the organization and knowledge of the employees enabled the job to be completed in a safe and efficient manner. For example, as many as 100 trains a day operated over the railway between Moncton, Truro and Halifax with as many as 22 trains moving safely and smoothly at one time over a stretch of 65 miles.

That same organization and skill has continued to provide excellent passenger service for Canada in the last 30 years since 1945.

During the first few years after World War II, CN began slowly but surely to recuperate after the exhausting task. Some equipment was rebuilt and a few new cars were ordered, but not many. Several new types of problems were beginning to plague the railway industry. Inflation and increased competition from air, bus and the private automobile began to make themselves felt more intensely than ever before. And then on June 25, 1950, the Korean War broke out and again Canadian National was called upon to move war materials and troops in great numbers. It almost seemed as though the railways would never be able to catch up with time.

However Canadian National was up to the task because of positive attitudes on the part of the management and employees who were proud to be part of the Canadian National team.

By 1951 CN began conducting several changes in operating techniques and service. They had had experience with diesel electric motor cars previously and this led to a 1951 branch line experiment. A diesel rail car was rebuilt with a new 400 horsepower, 12 cylinder Caterpillar diesel engine. This was enough power to pull two trailers. The motor car also contained baggage facilities behind the engine compartment. The matching trailer cars were also thoroughly modernized and included Rail Post Office space and accommodations for 44 passengers. The entire train was rebuilt with a streamlined appearance. The assignment for the train was a local run from Hamilton to Allandale. From there the train operated to Meaford and return and finally back to Hamilton, a total distance of 287 miles with but one man in the cab. The experiment attracted passengers for awhile, but the automobile eventually killed the train service.

While this was going on, CN was conducting studies for the purchase of new equipment. However the car builders were so heavily backlogged that orders were as much as two to three years behind. The CN decided against jumping on the "order" bandwagon until it was determined just what the public wanted and would pay for. This would eventually lead to the largest passenger car order ever placed. It was truly equipment marketing research in every sense of the word.

In the meantime, however, CN was quietly rebuilding passenger equipment. In 1952, for example, 20 tourist sleepers were rebuilt at the Transcona shops at Winnipeg at a cost of $16,000 each. The window center posts were removed from each pair of windows in the sections and a double glazed metal framed picture window four feet long put in its place. Mirrors were relocated alongside each of the seats, and an improved air conditioning unit placed over the center of each window.

THE NEW YORK-Philadelphia and Toronto "Maple Leaf" departs the Sunnyside Station en route to Toronto. This train was a joint CN-Lehigh Valley operation and included CN and LV equipment as well as Pullman cars. Indeed the Pullman next to the LV combine is the Illinois Central's Beach Grove, a 12 roomette, 2 single bedroom, 1 double bedroom and 1 drawing room sleeping car.

Elmer Treloar

LOCAL PASSENGER TRAIN No. 168, shown here at Stratford, Ontario, and its running mates 169, 170 and 171 provided a morning and afternoon local service between Stratford and Palmerston during the 1950's with through connections to London and Owen Sound.

Elmer Treloar

One of the interesting things about CN tourist sleepers is that they carried kitchen accommodations for the use of passengers in preparing meals. During the rebuilding process the kitchens were redone in Monel metal with a fast heating two burner hot plate replacing the former stove. The cars were also equipped with roller bearings and redecorated in pastel shades of green. They were placed in service on the Continental Limited, which by this time was the only transcontinental train operating between Toronto, Montreal and Vancouver, although the train did run in separate sections from the eastern cities.

Most of the passenger equipment study was completed by early 1952, and CN requested bids for 194 passenger cars at one time. That came as a shock to the railroad industry, but the bid request was only the beginning. The year 1953 arrived and CN placed orders for a total of 302 cars including a single order with Pullman for 92 sleeping cars, 17 parlor cars and combination parlor and meal service cars, 12 combination sleeping and meal service cars and 20 full dining cars. A total of 161 coaches were ordered from Canadian Car & Foundry. However that still wasn't enough and by the end of 1953, an additional 57 coaches were ordered and 30 baggage cars from National Steel Car Corporation at Hamilton. A grand total of 389 cars were ordered for the largest single order for passenger equipment ever placed in one year by one road in North America. The cost was in excess of $60 million, and few people could believe it.

The 218 coaches were built by CC&F and were identical. This technique provided CC&F with an unusual opportunity to reduce costs through stan-dardized production techniques. This was one of the results of the passenger equipment study. Yet people still could not understand why CN would make such an investment in passenger equipment. CNR President Donald Gordon and Railway Age magazine (March 22, 1954, p. 75) pointed out several reasons why CN ordered such a large amount of equipment.

When the war was over, CN needed to enter the market for equipment but large scale purchases had to wait. First an industrial boom (totally unexpected) absorbed steel at a high rate. Car builders consequently could not undertake the production of needed equipment. The industrial boom in turn caused a rise in freight traffic and so, secondly, available funds and materials had to be invested in freight cars and locomotives instead of passenger equipment. A third reason was that CN was denied increases in rates to keep in step with inflation, and for many years they moved a substantial amount of freight on substandard rates set down in the statute books in dollars and cents and unchanged for more than half a century. (And the US roads thought they were alone in the world with their problems with the ICC.) These problems kept the road from making the purchases required, and the 170 rebuilt cars (the rebuilding program mentioned previously) provided only a partial solution to the problem.

The passenger equipment study went on for nearly three years. They even went to the traveling public and asked directly through questionnaires what they wanted and would be willing to pay for.

20

TRAIN NO. 29 ARRIVES at the Sunnyside Station, Toronto en route from Toronto to London on a morning run which includes an overnight sleeper from Montreal. In addition to the head-end traffic and three coaches, 29 also carried a buffet parlor car. The nine car train was photographed August 6, 1957.

Elmer Treloar

As the study drew to its conclusion, the road discovered that it had a choice of being functional or fancy. It could have developed a glamor type of service on a few of its most important runs, or it could provide reasonably fast, comfortable service on all principal trains without expensive frills. As everyone knows now, the road chose to be functional or in other words, to get as much modern equipment as possible for the money and spread throughout the system so that the maximum number of passengers could benefit from them.

The new equipment also introduced the black-gold-green color scheme, which was undoubtedly one of the finest schemes ever developed. It did not show the dirt, and furthermore the inclusion of the maple leaf linked the CN most effectively with Canada.

When assigning the new cars, CN held to the goal of spreading the benefits as widely as possible. In addition to the mainliners, i.e., Montreal-Halifax, Montreal-Chicago, Toronto-Vancouver, etc., the assignments included many trains carrying but one sleeping car. Therefore one of the first sleepers was placed in service on January 23, 1954 on the 317 mile run between Montreal and Chicoutimi. This route serves the mining, paper making and aluminum processing "North Country" at the head of the Saguenay River.

This type of service need required that many different kinds of facilities be packed into one car with the emphasis on low cost space. That was why 52 of the sleepers combined open sections, double bedrooms and duplex roomettes; and 20 others combined sections, double bedrooms and roomettes. Ten of the sleepers combined sections and

bedroom space with eating facilities. Eleven of the parlor cars were arranged for meal service.

CN's investigations revealed that most of the traveling public thought that dining car prices were too high, and that they were willing to forego frills and large portions in favor of keeping prices down. Thus CN purchased 6 dinette cars which were equipped to either supplement full dining cars or to service a complete train load. These lunch counters were designed to serve full meals of the simpler variety, and to be available for snack during most of the day and evening.

Since there was no one train to celebrate, or a date of delivery (the cars arrived at the rate of 1 or 2 per week from the different builders for several months), the publication of the new equipment was more complicated than say it was for the Canadian on the Canadian Pacific. To get around this problem, CN printed up booklets and leaflets describing the various cars in both French and English. They also advertised extensively in U.S. and Canadian magazines and newspapers.

The equipment was displayed at various stations and terminals from time to time as it was delivered, as well as having radio and TV previews in Montreal, Toronto and Winnipeg before going into service.

Pullman-Standard constructed a total of 141 cars for Canadian National in 13 different floor plans, which incorporated the latest ideas in room arrangement and equipment for conventional parlor car and sleeping car travel as well as special dining facilities and business car service.

The full sleeping cars consisted of 52 four bedroom, four section, eight duplex roomette cars

THE INTERNATIONAL LIMITED en route from Chicago to Toronto pauses at 7:09 AM, right on time at Brantford, Ontario. No. 14 will arrive in Toronto at 8:55 AM and will continue to Montreal at 9:15 AM as a Canadian National-Canadian Pacific pool train. The consist of this joint GTW-CN train includes Railway Express Refers and several Pullmans from Chicago, including a Union Pacific sleeper from the Pullman pool. The photo was taken on May 15, 1955.
Elmer Treloar

(known as a 4-8-4 configuration); 20 six roomette, four bedroom, six section cars (known as a 6-4-6 configuration); 6 five bedroom, ten roomette cars (known as a 10-5 configuration); and 6 five compartment, three drawing room cars (known as a 5-3 configuration).

The four buffet sleeping dining cars were designed for low cost travel and included 8 open sections, one bedroom, and a 16 chair dining room served by a compact kitchen-pantry. The eight 2 compartment, 2 bedroom buffet lounge cars included a 36 foot lounge section seating 28 plus a separate porter's room. There were also six 10 section, one bedroom buffet cars in which there were spacious men's and women's dressing rooms.

The six parlor cars accommodated 34 passengers. The nine buffet parlor cars included one parlor section for 20 passengers plus a 16 seat dining alcove served by a compact kitchen-pantry. The two parlor buffet cars contained two parlor sections seating 7 and 15 respectively, plus an eight seat dining section and all purpose buffet.

The 14 dining cars seat 40 passengers with a 4-2 table arrangement. The six dinette cars contain a lunch counter extending for two-thirds of the length of the car and seat 26 passengers. There is a 13 foot kitchen with a back bar extending the full length of the counter. Dormitory quarters for six are included.

Probably the two most unusual cars of the order were the two seven compartment kitchen buffet lounge cars (with an open platform) arranged

as business or special purpose cars. Each car accommodates 14 passengers and a crew of two. The dual purpose buffet lounge room for eight is served by a compact kitchen that is fully equipped. To this writer's knowledge these were the last two cars constructed for private car service. Pullman maintained many such cars in the Pullman pool during the 1920's and 30's, but there are no such cars available in the U.S. at the present time for public use. The fact that the cars were built with open platforms makes them even more significant. They are, to this writer's knowledge, the last two cars ever built with open platforms for public use.

Privacy and comfort were emphasized in the construction of the various types of sleeping and parlor car equipment. The sleeping car plans were arranged so that the more expensive bedrooms, compartments and drawing rooms were near the center of the car for smoother riding. The room decorations included harmonious colors, soft carpeting and fine fabrics. The location of the triangular lavatory and dressing mirror inside the room (instead of in the annex) was and is a much desired convenience for dual room occupancy. Daytime travel was also improved by the use of two lounge type folding chairs in the bedrooms. These chairs could (and can) be moved to view the scenery, card playing, writing or eating meals and for just plain relaxation. The chairs are stored under the berths for night time occupancy.

The compartments and drawing rooms also contain these lounge type folding chairs as well as

22

CN PASSENGER TRAIN No. 168, the morning local from London to Palmerston, crosses the bridge at St. Marys, Ontario with a RPO-baggage, one coach and an express refer carrying the markers. The date is May 30, 1958.

Elmer Treloar

the full length convertible sofas. Compartments contain one chair while the drawing rooms have two.

Nearly all of these sleeping, dining and parlor cars are still in service.

The 218 air conditioned first class coaches were built by the Montreal plant of Canadian Car & Foundry. Each coach seats 80 passengers in a 52 passenger main section and a 28 seat smoking section. This method of separating the smokers from the non-smokers is actually a more economical idea than providing smoking lounge rooms at the ends of the passenger section, thereby sacrificing revenue space. It is an idea that Amtrak should pick up on, which in turn would increase the revenue space per car without sacrificing comfort.

The interior walls of the coaches were entirely without paint. Arborite, Panelyte or Dor-o-lam panels were applied to the ceiling, ends and sides. It is readily cleaned with soap and water and does not require repainting.

There were four color schemes originally employed on these cars: blue, rose, green and rust. All curtains were tan. Baggage racks extend the full length of the coach and are constructed of aluminum. All seats, except those at the bulkheads, were reclining and rotating with foot rests. Smoking section seats were fitted with recessed ashtrays. All seat cushions, backs and arm rests were of foam rubber and originally upholstered in textured wool frieze.

All of the coaches have been extensively rebuilt since their original construction. In fact all of the

389 cars written about in this section have gone through a refurbishing and the decor has been modified extensively. Indeed, the original black, gold and green with Maple Leafs has been replaced with a black and white scheme and a red-orange CN. Canadian National has has maintained the equipment in top-notch condition and it is very difficult to tell that the cars are now 21 years old.

Before we get too far ahead of ourselves, it should be mentioned that the CN invested heavily in rail diesel cars from the Budd Company from 1953 through 1959. Since that time additional cars have been purchased from the Boston & Maine. CN purchased all four types: RDC-1's, 2's, 3's and 4's plus the non-cab variety (Budd Company type RDC-9's) that are designated RDC-5's on CN. The first three cars were purchased in 1953, one RDC-1, one RDC-3 and one RDC-4. They were successfully tested on several routes and the customer reaction was positive. Originally the cars were purchased with the flip over or walk seats, or shall we say "off the shelf" models from Budd. However, it was soon found that the equipment was suitable for longer type runs. From the late 1950's on to the present time, RDC's are holding down some tough schedules, and they are doing it with day in and day out on time performance. Appropriately named "Railiners" many of the cars have been rebuilt with reclining seats and snack bars. The Railiners have been able to cut expenses for many runs, and have in many cases retained and built up passenger patronage. They were a sound investment for Canadian National to make during the mid to late 1950's.

23

PASSENGER EXTRA 6167 East moves along with five cars of rail fans on a Toronto-Lindsay turn. The train was photographed south of Goodwood, Ontario on January 28, 1962.

Elmer Treloar

CN TRAIN NO. 101 passes Bayview Junction en route from Toronto to Niagara Falls. At Hamilton, the train will become 102. The consist includes a buffet parlor car plus a through 24 duplex roomette sleeper from Montreal.

George-Paterson Collection

INBOUD IN LATE morning hours from Owen Sound, Ontario comes train 172 through West Toronto behind Pacific 5250 which has a bit of modernity with the caseing above its pilot. The date is May, 1957.
Jim Scribbins

As the 1950's drew to a close, Canadian National was experiencing an $18 million out of pocket deficit. The company was anxious to reduce and eliminate this financial drain. The usual pattern of most railroads in this situation was to downgrade equipment, service, schedules and the employee morale. This situation existed in the United States for nearly 25 years until Amtrak took over, and the problem is a long way from being solved. However the usual procedure was not followed by Canadian National.

In early 1959, President Donald Gordon called in the Director of Public Relations, Mr. W. R. Wright, and asked him to assemble a committee that would study the passenger business. It was the second major study undertaken by Canadian National within one decade, and it can be said that no other railway in North America put as much time and effort into the passenger business. The task of the committee was to take a long look at publicity, advertising, promotional methods, pricing policies, equipment and equipment utilization, train schedules, customer relations, personnel training and meal and beverage service. Further, all of these items were to be studied in the light of the requirements and demands of the traveling public.

The result of this study launched the railway into a new era of passenger operations under the direction of Mr. Garth C. Campbell, who in various capacities (including General Manager of Passenger Sales and Service) lead the project from 1961 through 1968. Mr. Campbell is now CN's newest Vice President of CN's newest department, Passenger Marketing. This new era has now continued for 15 years, and with the exception of

Auto-Train, no other service has been so positively operated.

One of the first results of the study was the now World famous Red, White and Blue fares. Here for the first time was a fare structure that varied according to the degree of the demand. In other words prices were differentiated on the basis of high, medium and low periods of travel. The highest prices were charged on the days or periods of time with the highest demand and so on. The new fare structure was first placed into operation between Montreal and the Maritimes on April 23, 1962. On October 27, 1963, the plan was extended across Canada. The result was an increase in passenger patronage. For example, during the first year of operation east of Montreal, passenger miles increased 46%. The Super Continental's first month on Red, White and Blue fares resulted in a 67% increase in passenger miles and an 18% increase in revenue. This type of increase was experienced system wide, and the system has been successful. As we roll through the 1970's, the system remains in effect.

Simply changing the fare structure, however, would not attract and retain passengers. The committee had to determine what combination of fares, train schedules, equipment and personal services would attract passengers. Schedules were studied concerning speed, convenient hours, frequency and so forth. Equipment had to be attractive, comfortable, suitable, practical, functional and in a state of repair and cleanliness second to none. Personal services included everything that makes it easy and pleasant for the public to do business with railway personnel and a customer-oriented attitude which anticipates the needs and

THE FIREMAN APPEARS to be keeping a sharp eye on the photographer. Train 117, the Inter-City Limited from London and Toronto has just arrived at Windsor behing U-2-g 4-8-4 No. 6231 on a warm June, 1954 afternoon. The station has been replaced by a new one in the Walkerville district and a pre-served light Pacific occupies this approximate location. In the background is one of the Detroit River car ferries.

Jim Scribbins

desires of the passengers. This new philosophy was totally embraced by 1964, and although the committee has disbanded, CN continues to study and change the passenger services as the needs dictate. In fact during the past decade, CN has made many changes and improvements and readily admits that the job will never be done. Consequently this past decade has been one of the most exciting eras of passenger service on Canadian National. Let's take a look at some of these developments.

With the new Red, White & Blue fares, CN's passenger business began to expand and increase at a rapid rate. The company needed additional equipment, and they began to shop around in the United States. In 1964 CN purchased six of the Milwaukee Road Super Domes as well as the six Skytop Lounge sleeping cars which were renamed Skyview lounges. They also picked up a number of coaches and sleepers, but one of the more significant purchases was the Reading Railroad's Crusader. Purchased in early 1964, the five car streamliner was completely rebuilt and renamed the "Champlain."

The Champlain was a continuation of the positive passenger philosophy developed by the CN. The difference here though was that a new train was being placed in service on the short haul where competition with highways is the keenest. The Champlain began service on the Montreal—Quebec pool service with the Canadian Pacific in June, 1964. The new train cut the running time substantially over the 170 mile run. The schedule of three hours, fifteen minutes was 30 minutes faster than the next fastest train. This was accomplished by operating at 80 miles per hour and eliminating all intermediate stops except

one at suburban Ste. Foy, just outside of Quebec City.

The consist of the Champlain remained the five stainless steel cars built by the Budd Company in the mid-1930's. Two of the cars were refurbished with a 64 coach seating capacity. Two of the other coaches were rebuilt with 39 passenger parlor car 2-1 seating. The center car of the consist retained its diner lounge configuration. Both coach and parlor car seats were sold on a reserved basis. Stewards were in attendance in all cars and a public address system provided music and announcements in both French and English. Other extras included free pillows and receptacles between each pair of seats to accommodate beverages. With the Red, White and Blue fares passengers were able to save as much as 40% off the original fares.

The Champlain was eventually replaced by a Rapido train, which now makes the run in two hours, fifty nine minutes. The Rapido was placed in service in early 1967. Meanwhile, the Champlain equipment was farmed out to other runs and split up.

The Panorama was also introduced on the transcontinental run in April, 1964. The new train carried top-notch equipment with the same service as the Super Continental.

The year 1965 brought about an end to the passenger train pool service between Montreal-Toronto, and Montreal-Quebec City. This ended an arrangement that had lasted for 32 years, which was brought about initially to improve service but yet reduce costs during the Depression. The pool service trains operated with a mixture of CP and CN equipment. In early 1966 Canadian National announced that a new agreement had been reached with the Canadian Pacific. CP discontinued all passenger service between Toronto and Montreal and also on the Toronto-Ottawa run. Canadian National now provides the only rail passenger service between the three points, and operates over CP trackage between Smith Falls and Brockville.

The year 1968 saw the arrival of the Turbo-Trains, but due to technical difficulties the trains did not see regular service until after 1972. The Turbo's and another concept in train service equipment, the Tempo's (which were ordered in 1966 from Hawker Siddeley of Canada Limited) were the result of still further studies by CN's passenger traffic department, operating department and research and development.

The Tempo trains operate between Windsor, Sarnia and Toronto. Altogether 25 cars were delivered in 1967 and included 15 coaches, five cafe coaches and five club cars. It was about 1967 when CN changed the name of parlor cars to club cars. The Tempo trains operate in either 4 or 5 car sets of 3 coaches, 1 cafe coach and a club car on some runs. The interior decor and on board services were styled after the Turbo-Trains.

The Turbo's are now (1975) operating on a double daily schedule between Toronto and Montreal and Montreal and Ottawa. The Turbo's (trains 63, 67, 62, 66) are scheduled for 4 hours, 10 minutes for the 335 mile Montreal-Toronto run, the fastest schedule ever for the route. Previous to this the Rapidos were the fastest with a 4 hour, 59 minute schedule. The Montreal-Ottawa Turbo service began in 1974 with a 1 hour, 49 minute schedule for the 115 mile operation. At the present time, Turbos are limited to 95 miles per hour top speed.

Passenger service continues to improve on Canadian National as we move through the 1970's. CN and CP have made some preliminary studies concerning the operation of passenger trains throughout Canada. As a result, Canadian Pacific is now a user of CN's electronic computer system for reservations on the Canadian and Atlantic Limited.

Since the early 1970's, CN has spent more than $10 million refurbishing equipment, and they have led the way in pioneering meal service. For example, the passenger department has come up with four new concepts in food and beverage service. These are in service on various trains throughout Canada. Such equipment includes Snack Bar Lounge cars with electric ovens for heating sandwiches and various types of light meals. Cafe Bar Lounge cars have also been introduced on such trains as the Rapido and runs to Windsor. This type of a car is equipped with micro-wave ovens and is stocked with frozen meals that are ¾ cooked. The newest innovation in meal service is the Cafe Lounge car which provides take out service, sit down meal service and lounge service. Cafe lounge cars are equipped with infrared ovens for frozen meals.

Aside from dining and dinette cars, there are two other developments for meal and beverage service. One of these is the snack coach which

OVERNIGHT TRAIN NO. 33 to Winnipeg loads express and passengers prior to departure from Port Arthur (now Thunder Bay North). The date is June 10, 1952 and the consist of one combine, two coaches and one sleeper will be doubled at Fort Frances where the Duluth-Winnipeg cars are added to 33's consist.

Elmer Treloar

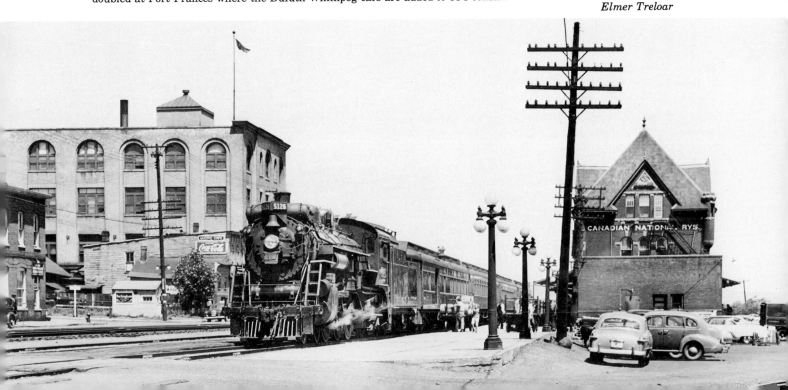

provides sandwiches and drinks and is equipped with a cooler. Some rail diesel cars are equipped with such facilities. The other type of car is the club galley. This type of parlor car service includes meals at one's seat, and the kitchen or galley is equipped with a convection oven. This oven is a sealed chamber with rapid high heat with air forced around the product to be heated.

Canadian National also operates dining cars on such trains as the Super Continental, Ocean and Scotion. Dinette cars operate on these trains and others such as the Rapido and trains to Chicoutimi.

The $10 million refurbishing program also included the complete modernization of the Sceneramic dome cars for the Rockies, lounge cars, Dayniter coaches and sleeping cars. The dome cars included new seating arrangements to provide easier visiting for groups and for viewing the scenery. The Dayniter coaches include leg rest seats and individual tables for each seat. The sleeping cars include more modern arrangements and appointments all designed to make it the last word in sleeping car comfort. The refurbished cars have been decorated in reds, blacks, blues, purples, greens and a variety of colors all designed to complement each other to make travel restful and attractive.

Equipment alone has not been the sole objective in the continuous modernization program.

DOUBLE HEADED SKI TRAIN departs Winnipeg for Snow Valley, Manitoba on January 4, 1951.

Stan F. Styles

Train tickets, for example, have evolved from the vertical ticket, which could be 3 or 4 feet long for long journeys, to vertical ticket booklets and finally to the easy to understand horizontal ticket.

Canadian National and Amtrak now exchange reservations by permitting each other access to the reservation computers and this in turn, increases the number of sales outlets on both sides.

In Chapter 3, we will talk about the Auto-With-You plan, which as of early 1975 is only operated during the summer months. However, Canadian National offers an all year round auto service with Car-Go-Rail. Here autos are carried in fast time freights while the passenger(s) travel aboard passenger trains. The Car-Go-Rail service is available between Halifax, Moncton, Montreal, Toronto, Winnipeg, and Saskatoon, Edmonton and Vancouver. CN earned approximately $1.7 million in net income in 1972 and 1973, and 1974 recorded a visible increase in Car-Go-Rail traffic.

Canadian National has continued to expand the various type of incentive fares, which were introduced in the early 1960's with the three level Red, White and Blue fares discussed earlier in this chapter. For example, CN has discounts for youth travel, senior citizen travel and family and group fares. Another incentive fare is the Canrail pass for U.S. and European residents which allows up to a month's travel time anywhere in Canada on any train.

THE TRI-WEEKLY TRAIN, No. 16, from Prince Albert, Sask., Swan River and Dauphin arrives at Portage la Prairie en route to Winnipeg on August 31, 1950. Note the number and variety of express refers on the head-end of this double header from the Canadian North.

Stan F. Styles

BRANCH LINE LOCAL passenger trains were once far more numerous all over CN's far flung system. The consist varied from assignment to assignment, but one thing was always certain, the cars were old and most likely wooden. Here we see the local from the Gypsumville line north of Winnipeg heading for that city on the open prairie in December, 1940. The consist is a little bigger than one might expect, but then again the run was longer too. The Ten Wheeler looks very much at home on this quaint little train.

Stan F. Styles

Another fare innovation is the tour package. This includes the "Maple Leafe Package Tours" which are deluxe, independent, unescorted tours from Montreal, Toronto, Winnipeg and Vancouver. The package rate includes train and hotel accomodations, meals at selected points and a wide variety of sightseeing packages by motor coach.

A second type of tour is the "Maple Leaf Invitation" tours which are sold beyond the peak summer month travel season. These offer city accommodations with sightseeing tours. These tours are offered to Winnipeg, Edmonton, Vancouver, Victoria, Halifax, Quebec, Montreal, Ottawa, Toronto and Niagara Falls.

To this writer's knowledge, Canadian National is the only railway to offer "Air/Rail" tours. These

are available to US visitors and consist of Air Canada air service from US points to rail gateway cities with tour marketing through both Air Canada and Canadian National passenger sales offices.

The most unusual tour is the "Hudson Bay Explorers" trip which is an all-expense trip from Winnepeg to Churchill, Manitoba on Hudson Bay. The train is the passenger's home for the entire trip including the six day special tour and five day explorer tours. If a passenger wishes to go further north, he can fly an air tour to Rankin Inlet 300 miles north of Churchill in the Northwest Territories.

Although Canadian National service nationwide is important, the most crucial and heaviest

TRAIN NO. 4, the Continental, overtakes an extra east in CTC territory at Oba, Ontario on October 26, 1958. At the right edge of the photo are gons of the Algoma Central which crosses the CNR at this still rather remote community.

Jim Scribbins

0-6-0 STEAM SWITCHER No. 7303 heads for the repair shops at Winnipeg with a 24 duplex roomette sleeper and a dining car in March, 1951. The sleeper was one of 20 such cars bulilt by Canadian Car and Foundry in 1949, and were the first streamlined sleepers on CN. The cars are known as the "I" series with such names as Indigo, Iris, Irma, Irondale, Iroquois and others. The equipment rides on six wheeled trucks and has provided many services such as tourist roomettes and dormettes.

Stan F. Styles

TRAIN NO. 19, a virtual all-stop local between Campbellton and Montreal was the remnant of the Maritime Express. In the rain at Riviere-du-Loup, Quebec, mail and express are put aboard while the pair of MLW's gurgle in their individual contented way. Behind the two head-end cars are two coaches (streamlined and semi-streamlined) and a standard diner in which the hospitable staff will soon prepare a hot lunch to warm the somewhat chilled rail cameraman Jim Scribbins. The date is September 30, 1966.

IN THE LATE 1950's, there was operated ahead of the Continental, a mail and express train No. 103, which halted for the most part only at crew change points between Capreol and Winnipeg. A GP-9 with Flexicoil trucks and a steam generator car held down the head-end, while a combine, in which the friendly conductor and flagman brewed good strong tea for the passengers as well as for themselves, carried the markers. The scene is at Foleyet, Ontario during an engine crew change in October, 1958.

Jim Scribbins

area of travel is the Windsor – Sarnia, Toronto, Montreal (including Ottawa) and Quebec corridor. This area or strip of geography contains the greatest concentration of Canada's population. It is in this area, the 335 mile run between Montreal and Toronto, that the Turbo averages 80 miles per hour for the entire trip. At this point in time (January, 1975), the Turbo has not realized its full potential in terms of speed, but it gives us a hint of the future.

By the time this book is in print by September, 1975, Canadian National will have formulated, or

at least be well on the way, to making new announcements concerning expanded, new different types of passenger service. Contrary to some newspaper articles already published, the Super Continental will not be discontinued as such and replaced with a series of day trains. However a new day train service concept is part of planning now going on. Other new plans include integrated rail-bus services, new ticketing and reservation concepts, new pricing ideas and various types of new train service proposals.

CN PASSENGER UNITS 6765 and 6865 (Montreal Locomotive Works Type FPA-4's and FPB-4's) are regarded among some fans as being the most attractive road power on the rails. The 6765 and 6865 are shown here in the original "Maple Leaf" color scheme of olive green, black and golden yellow. Note the bell on top and the chimes horn.

Canadian National

WHILE THE CONDUCTOR confers with the engine crew, passengers move along the platform to their respective car locations. The two GMD's and MLW FPA-4 will lead the impressive consist of the Ocean, train No. 15, out of Halifax this September 28, 1966.

Jim Scribbins

PROBABLY THE MOST unusual engines used in passenger train service are these General Electric 600 hp, 70 ton units ready to depart from Charlottetown, Prince Edward Island with train 115 to Moncton, New Brunswick. The date is September 29, 1966.

Jim Scribbins

TRAIN NO. 15, the Ocean, eases away from the depot at Sackville, New Brunswick on September 28, 1966. Bringing up the rear is Skyview sleeper Fundy (ex-Milwaukee Road Skytop Coffee Creek), and ahead of the all time great lounge sleeper are two sleepers, sleeper lounge car, diner, two more lightweight sleepers, then three heavy weight 12-1's serving as "dormette" cars, a standard diner, streamlined coaches, coach-lounge car and a pair of head-end cars.

Jim Scribbins

In the meantime, passengers are seeing new passenger train crew uniforms, hot food and beverage on wheeled carts that travel through the trains, and of course the continuation of such train service as ski trains. In fact, as this is being written the popular weekend ski train, the "Winter Wonderland Special" will resume operations for eight weekends between Edmonton and Jasper beginning January 24 through March 14, 1975. The train is now in its fourth season, and it has gained so much popularity that some trains are heavily booked months in advance, and one additional trip was added for the 1975 season.

Skiers making the trip are charged $60 which includes rail fare, transfer to and from Jasper Park Lodge, two nights accomodation, bus transportation to and from Marmot Basin and lift tickets for two days of skiing. Non-skiers pay $43 with lower rates for children.

AT EMERALD JUNCTION, PEI. the passenger train from the capital made connections with mixed trains from the western part of the island. Business was good for CN in the Summer of 1966 and it borrowed several Canadian Pacific coaches including this one bringing up the rear of No. 115. The three little GE's remained on the sharply curved (originally narrow gauge) confines of the former PEI Ry., while the coach and head-end and steam generator cars were taken across Northhumberland Strait on a CN ferry. In New Brunswick, the train was pulled by a MLW RS-18.

Jim Scribbins

The Winter Wonderland Special includes an entertainment car with a sing-along piano. Very few such trains include such a car, but we find one on a combination Canadian National, Central Vermont-Amtrak train in the east, a train that also carries skiers. That car is known as Le Pub and operates on trains 26 and 27, the Montrealer between Montreal and White River Junction and beyond.

CN passenger service is offered over every important line in Canada. In all instances, equipment is clean and well maintained. Amtrak has been carefully studying CN passenger operations, and they have been importing techniques and service innovations. Canadian National track in the main lines is in superb condition, and the research and development department continues to search for new and smoother ways of operating passenger and freight trains. In fact, that department is very extensively involved in studies concerning not

IN JUNE, 1970, THERE was what could be described as an up-dated version of a mail and express train operated between Montreal and Winnipeg, and here, arriving at its terminal a few minutes to the good is train No. 7: GP-9, steam generator, head-end cars, one coach and a standard 12 section, 1 drawing room sleeper, the Peterborough.

Jim Scribbins

TRAIN 192 DEPARTS WINNIPEG for Port Arthur in June, 1969. The dome of the CN station (sometimes referred to as Union Station, and originally the Fort Garry Station) is to the left and the Railway's Fort Garry Hotel is the dignified building to the right. Since this June 1969 day, the train's number has been changed and RDC's replaced the locomotive and cars, and the eastern terminal is now Thunder Bay North.

Jim Scribbins

BEARING DOWN ON the photographer is the only passenger train (at the time) not stopping at suburban Dorval, Quebec: Rapido train No. 65. The consist includes three GMD "F" units and 10 cars the last one of which carries the train's name lettered boldly on its flank.

Jim Scribbins

only the Tempos, the Turbos but also the LRC. The LRC will be described in Chapter 15, Research and Development, which is a very important part of CN's corporate structure.

It could be said that CN passenger services are unequaled anywhere in North America, with the possible exception of Auto-Train.

Before we close this chapter it might be well to take a look at a number of passenger trains that have carried on traditions of good service and good will for Canadian National for many years. There are a number of such trains that continue to offer the finest of services.

The Ocean and the Scotian are the fleet leaders east of Montreal. Operating between Montreal and Halifax, they carry a full compliment of accommodations and are similar in many ways to the Super Continental. Prior to the mid-1950's, the Ocean Limited was one of Canada's All-Sleeping car trains but with stiff automobile competition she

lost that distinction. The Ocean also carries through cars to and from Sydney.

The Cavalier is the overnight Montreal-Toronto passenger train in that heavily travelled corridor. She is usually assigned two sleepers and at least four coaches during normal traffic periods. Prior to the Rapidos and Turbos and other high speed day trains, it was not uncommon for the Cavalier to operate in two sections as an all-sleeping car section and an all coach section. At the present time, a snack bar lounge is operated in the train, which also carries mail cars one of a few trains in Canada to do so.

The Northland has a romantic ring and is one of a few dual railway operations. The Northland operates between Toronto, North Bay, Noranda, Timmins and Kapuskasing. The train operates over the CN to North Bay, the Ontario Northland to Cochrane and finally the CN again to Kapus-kasing. Through sleepers and coaches operate to all points, and there is an added feature of a joint Ontario Northland—Canadian National power pool. ONR FP-7's in their beautiful green and yel-

AT THE WESTERN END of CN's most intensive passenger service area, train 146 awaits the highball from Windsor to Toronto. This train was usually composed of the silver Tempo stock, but this day the somewhat rare FP-4 units afforded some compensation for the lack of ultra-modern equipment, and the ride was quite pleasant and on time. September 11, 1971.

Jim Scribbins

IMMEDIATELY FOLLOWING 65 comes train 55, the Bonaventure which has its FPA's (which are capable of 92 miles per hour) spliced by a GMD "F" unit and consisting of 9 cars. The date is September 20, 1966.

Jim Scribbins

THE CABOT (trains 18 and 19) was an extra streamliner for world fair traffic between Montreal and Sydney during Expo 67. A complete selection of accommodations were available to passengers.

Canadian National

low can be found at the Toronto coach yards between assignments on 87 and 88.

There are countless other trains too. For example the nameless trains between Quebec, Senneterre and Cochrane or Montreal and Chicoutimi. These trains continue to operate without the fan fare of the Tempo, Turbos or the Super Continental. Yet Canadian National spares nothing in providing excellent equipment on these routes.

It is difficult to sum up CN's passenger services in one chapter, or even three chapters, in a book of this nature. Many trains have been left out simply because of a lack of space. CN passenger services deserve a book all of their own just for the last 15 years.

Before closing this chapter, it must be pointed out that there is an atmosphere aboard Canadian National passenger trains that one does not find elsewhere. It is difficult to explain the atmosphere,

but it is a cozy one in which it makes it very easy to relax. It is an atmosphere that beckons people to return again and again to travel as guests on board CN's superb passenger fleet. The fleet that is led by one of North America's finest trains, the Super Continental, which is what Chapter 3 is all about.

As we go to press, new developments are taking place with Canadian National's passenger services. A great deal of research is now being undertaken and the results are already hitting the rails. In February, 1975 CN announced a new incentive fare plan that reduced round trip fares between some cities as much as 33 per cent.

This new plan is designed to promote off-peak travel and release needed train space for business people who must travel at peak times. As of April, 1975, the plan was proving very effective.

The new fare structure differentiates fares by time of day, just as the red, white and blue plan relates travel cost to days of the week. It was initially applied to trains operating in the territory extending from Mont Joli, Quebec to Windsor, Ontario. Included are trains out of Toronto to Windsor, Sarnia, Niagara Falls, Ottawa and Montreal. All trains scheduled out of Montreal to Ottawa, Quebec City and Mont Joli also qualify as do all intermediate stations, provided the regular one-way red fare is $5.00 or more.

To qualify for the new fares, a passenger must purchase a round trip ticket and complete his travel within a four day period. Rather than paying the full round trip fare, he or she is charged the regular blue fare between the two cities plus one third. A further stipulation requires that the trains on which the passenger travels do not begin their runs between 4:00 and 6:30 PM. The fare structure is designed to influence travel patterns to better serve all travel markets and improve equipment utilization.

For passengers wishing to travel from any point outside the discount territory to a point within the territory or vice-versa a reduced fare applies for that portion of the journey within the designated area.

THE WINNIPEG-CHURCHILL train No. 93 pauses at Dauphin, Manitoba in the 10:00 PM dusk of a June evening in 1969.

Jim Scribbins

The new fare structure or reduction is just one more of the many positive actions carried out by CN that demonstrates the Railway is interested in the future of passenger train travel, and in attracting larger numbers of Canadians to travel by rail.

LE CHAMPLAIN WAS the Reading Railroad's Crusader described in Chapter 5 of *Coach Trains & Travel*. When purchased by CN, she originally operated as a CN-CP pool train between Montreal and Quebec City. Later she was replaced by Rapido trains, and now the equipment is split up, but the memory of the smart little all-coach streamliner lives on. Prior to going into service on CN, parlor car seats were added to the accommodations.

Canadian National

CN PASSENGER TRAIN No. 145, the "Tempo" has just arrived at Windsor, Ontario with a MLW 1800 hp road switcher leading three coaches and one club galley car. The road switcher's red color scheme goes well with the stainless steel passenger equipment.

Patrick C. Dorin

THE "CHURCHILL" TRAINS meet at the passing track designated in the timetable at Pipun, Manitoba. Southbound 92 rolls by on the main with a business car carrying its markers. The tripod type line poles are used the entire distance between The Pas and Churchill because of soil conditions. Notice how slender the trees are.

Jim Scribbins

TRAIN 93 EN ROUTE to Churchill stands at the division point of The Pas, Manitoba at breakfast time. Ahead lies an approximately 24 hour run to Hudson Bay.

Jim Scribbins

TRAINS 92 AND 93 are the link with Winnipeg for all the territory north of The Pas bringing groceries and all other necessities of life. Quite expectedly, local residents turn out to greet them, as in this case of 93 at Thicket Portage, Manitoba.
Jim Scribbins

WHEN THE MINING city of Thompson was established a few years ago, CN constructed a 31 mile branch line and the tri-weekly Churchill trains make the side trip regularly. (Trains 90 and 91 operate a Winnipeg-Thompson service the alternate days.) This is 93 re-entering the main line from the branch at Sipiwesk, Manitoba. Several of the box express cars carrying the supplies of daily living will be set out at stations along the way before terminating in the sub-arctic the next morning.
Jim Scribbins

TRAIN 93, FROM WINNIPEG, has just arrived at Churchill. An hour or so later, the sun disappeared and throughout the afternoon a wet sticky snow fell. A connection was made to the station building's heat system to obtain steam for the cars during their layover. The Eskimo Museum is within easy walking distance of the railway station as are restaurants and local stores.
Jim Scribbins

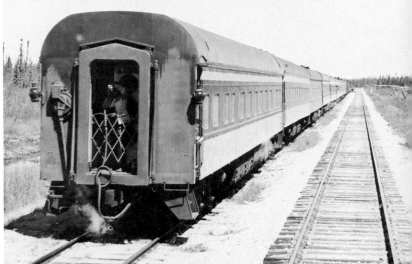

THE PHOTOGRAPHER JIM Scribbins was being photographed from 93, which is in the hole at Pipum as seen from 92 en route to Winnipeg in June, 1969.

CN's GAS ELECTRIC car No. 15882, shown here at Halifax, Nova Scotia on August 9, 1957, was repainted with streamlined colors of green and golden yellow complete with Maple Leafs.
Elmer Treloar

THE 1951 DIESEL ELECTRIC car experiment for the Hamilton-Allendale run was often tried on other routes for customer reaction and other reasons. On March 12, 1953 she handled a mixed train's run (M391 and 394) between Beeton and Collingwood, Ontario. The three car streamlinerette is shown here at Collingwood at 12:45 PM. Note the CNR Maple Leaf emblem on the nose of the train, which was painted green and golden yellow.
Elmer Treloar

WHEN THIS PHOTO was taken in July, 1963 at Kelowna, British Columbia, RDC-3 No. D-354 was assigned to the Kelowna-Kamloops Junction run, a distance of 118.9 miles. By 1964, the run was replaced by a bus service. Note the extra portable headlights for better visability around curves.

Harold K. Vollrath Collection

CANADIAN NATIONAL STILL operates RDC-4's in service nation wide, but the RPO section no longer serves its original function and the word "mail" has been removed from the sides of all RDC-4's.

Harold K. Vollrath Collection

RAILINER TRAIN NO. 687 departs Neebing en route to Winnipeg on its tri-weekly (686 is the eastbound side of this run) trip. The two car local takes 12 hours, 15 minutes to complete the 438 mile run. The RDC-1 leads en route to Winnipeg, while the RDC-4 is the head-end to Thunder Bay.

Patrick C. Dorin

CN's TURBO EQUIPMENT is made up of three 9 car sets. Each train consists of two power dome cars (one with 30 club seats and the other with 28 coach seats and 24 lounge seats) and seven cars offering club, coach and cafe service for a grand total of 372 passengers. Turbos now (1975) serve double daily assignments Montreal-Toronto and also between Montreal and Ottawa.

Canadian National

THE BISTRO CAR was a highly successful venture on the Rapido between Montreal and Toronto. With its well stocked bar and a lively piano player, many a passenger said later that he stood at the bar all the way from Toronto to Montreal and enjoyed every minute of it.

Canadian National

REFRESHMENT WAGONS BRING sandwiches and favorite beverages to Turbocoach passengers.

Canadian National

CN's STEAM MOTIVE power fleet consists of one 4-8-2 steam locomotive No. 6060 for fan and excursion passenger train service.

Canadian National

THE 6060 WITH WHITE flags flying powers a rail fan trip complete with a baggage recreation car for tape recorders, etc. This photo brings back many memories and really, what more can be said?

Canadian National

CN HAS EXPERIMENTED with new ways of food service. One result is the Cafe Bar Lounge car. Such cars are equipped with three sections, a coach lounge area (shown here) with coach seats and tables, a serving bar area and a refreshment lounge. Each of the two lounge areas can be used for either eating or drinking your favorite refreshment. Cafe Bar Lounge cars are numbered in the 2500-2511 series.

Canadian National

FOOD AT THE serving bar is displayed in this glass enclosed refrigerator. To this writer's knowledge, such a feature is not found on any other North American railroad.

Canadian National

CAFE BAR LOUNGE cars contain a micro-wave oven at the take out or serving bar area.

Canadian National

ANOTHER INNOVATION IS THE Cafe Lounge cars. These cars contain an informal dining room, coffee shop bar and lounge area. The cars, numbered 750 to 765, have separate lounge rooms away from the thru car traffic. The lounge is shown in this photo.

Canadian National

STILL ANOTHER INNOVATION in meal service is the serving of food at one's seat in club car service. Tables fold down from the seat ahead (which do not interfere with the reclining abilities of the seats). The steward serves the food on trays complete with a non-skid place mat. It is a very convenient service for club car passengers.

Canadian National

INTERIORS OF THE dinette cars (series 425-435) are highly attractive with the long "drug store" type bar extending the length of the dining room. Beyond the door in the right hand side of the photo is a hallway leading to the end of the car. That end of the car also contains a dormitory accommodation for two crew members.

Canadian National

DURING THE 1930's, CN purchased a fleet of coach equipment with exteriors similar to the cars built in quantity for the New Haven and other US roads. The 5227 is shown here at Chicago in October, 1964.

Jim Scribbins

COACH NO. 5284 is similar in many ways to the 5227 shown previously. This photo shows the new image black and white color scheme. The car was photographed at Chicago in October, 1964.

Jim Scribbins

THIS PHOTO SHOWS the interior of the type car described in the previous photo. Note the division of smoking and non-smoking compartments, a very worthwhile innovation that US roads should emulate more than they do now as it increases revenue seating.

Jim Scribbins

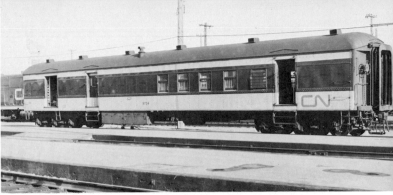

WIDE SPREAD USE of Rail Post Office cars was discontinued earlier in Canada than they were in the USA. This particular car, No. 9734, was photographed after being switched out of train No. 18 at Moncton, New Brunswick in September, 1966.

Jim Scribbins

THE FIRST STREAMLINED coaches ordered by CN came from Canadian Car and Foundry in 1947. The cars (series 5382 to 5411) were built with vestibules at both ends and six wheeled trucks, and were painted CN's olive green. 5404 was photographed by Stan F. Styles at Vancouver in May, 1954.

THE STREAMLINED ERA coaches built by Canadian Car & Foundry in 1954 contain 80 seats (split with the smoking and non-smoking sections), one men's lavatory at the vestibule end and a pair of women's lavatories at the blind end. The 5469 was photographed at Chicago on the Grand Trunk Western in October, 1964.

Jim Scribbins

THE CC&F BUILT coaches are the backbone of CN's coach fleet and now all wear the white and black with red-orange CN. This photo shows the 5542 in the consist of the Maple Leaf at Cassopolis, Michigan.

Sy Dykhouse

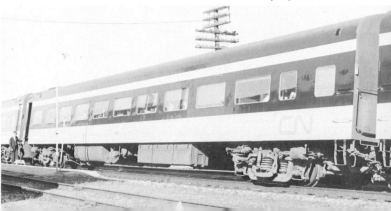

THIS PHOTO SHOWS the opposite side window configuration of the CC&F streamlined coaches.

Canadian National Collection

THE COMPLETE NUMBER series of this coach fleet ran from 5437 to 5654. All equipment contains separate smoking and non-smoking coach sections, reclining seats done up in a variety of colors and coat hooks above the windows.

Canadian National

CN PURCHASED A FLEET of coaches in 1968 for the new "Tempo" service between Sarnia, Windsor and Toronto. There were a total of 15 coaches (360 to 374), five cafe coaches (340 to 344) and five Club Galleys (320 to 324) built by Hawker-Siddeley at Thunder Bay, Ontario.

Patrick C. Dorin

CAFE COACH LOUNGE car No. 3028 (3009 to 3039) is equipped with three sections: 44 coach seats, serving bar and a 19 seat lounge section. Economical snack, light meals and beverages may be purchased in this equipment. These cars have replaced conventional dining cars on short distance trains with substantial success.

Canadian National

DINING CAR 1254 is typical of the olive green standard dining cars operated from the 1920's through the 1950's. Approximately 80 feet long, the cars provided seating for 30 passengers. The car was photographed in Vancouver in May, 1954.

Stan F. Styles

NOT ALL EQUIPMENT received such refurbishing. For example, dining car No. 1256 changed very little from the standard era, and its only claim to modernism is the black and white image and air conditioning. The car was photographed on train No. 93 at The Pas, Manitoba in June, 1969.

Jim Scribbins

A NUMBER OF dining cars, such as 1296, were refurbished and given "streamliner" type interiors and windows (with rounded corners) during the late 1950's. This also included the green and black color scheme complete with Maple Leafs.

Canadian National

THE STREAMLINED DINING cars were approximately 85 feet long and seat 48 passengers in the dining room. All dining cars now carry the black and white. The car was photographed at Jasper, Alberta in August, 1972.

Stan F. Styles

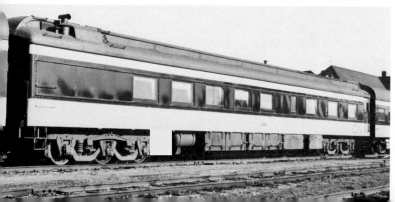

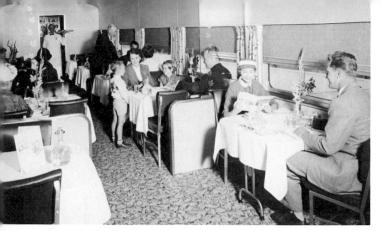

THIS PHOTO SHOWS a typical CN dining car interior.
Canadian National

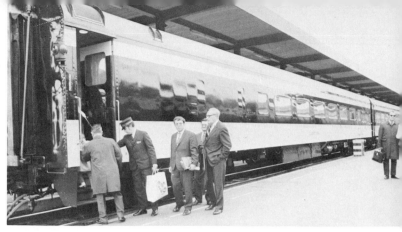

PARLOR CAR SERVICE is called "Club" car service on Canadian National Railways. Such service is offered in both full parlors or clubs, or what is known as Club Galleys. Club St. Denis is such a car which offers meal service within the car to club car passengers.

Canadian National

CLUB GALLEYS ARE equipped with special heating ovens to complete cooking. The steward is shown here placing trays of food into the ovens.

Canadian National

AFTER HEATING, THE food is served to passengers at their seats.

Canadian National

A GOOD DEAL of the club car seating on Canadian National is the popular 2-1 arrangement. Single seat comfort is maintained and at the same time the capacity of the car is substantially increased to 45 seats for full clubs, and to 38 seats for club galleys. Passengers are also served from food and beverage carts if they desire.

Canadian National

TEMPO CLUB GALLEY CAR rests between runs at Windsor, Ontario in September, 1971. Tempo clubs carry 2-1 seating for a total of 39 seats. The windowless area is a kitchen or galley. Note the small service door at floor level.

Jim Scribbins

CLUB CARS ALSO CONTAIN single seating, and tables are available for passengers.

Canadian National

ALMA LAKE IS a 38 seat club car rebuilt in 1947 from a hospital car.

Canadian National

GREAT SLAVE LAKE is a 45 seat club car, which was rebuilt from a lounge car in 1935.

Canadian National

TORONTO WAS TYPICAL of the heavy weight 12 section, 1 drawing room sleeping cars operated during the standard era. The car was olive green with gold lettering and was photographed at Prince George, British Columbia in May, 1954.

Stan F. Styles

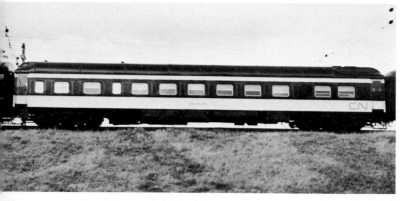

DALHOUSIE IS A modernized 12 section, 1 drawing room sleeping car, and equipment of this type is often operated in Toronto area CN suburban service.

Canadian National

WHYCOCOMAGH, ALSO A 12-1 car, shows the opposite side window configuration of Dalhousie shown previously. This car was photographed in Churchill service in June, 1969.

Jim Scribbins

BRANTFORD IS A modernized 8 section, 2 compartment and 1 drawing room sleeping car.

Canadian National

AMONG THE HUGE order of passenger equipment were the "E" series of sleepers. The cars contained 4 sections, 8 duplex roomettes and 4 double bedrooms. A typical example is the Erickson shown here in the handsome black and green scheme adopted at the time of purchase. Car was photographed at Vancouver in June, 1956.

Stan F. Styles

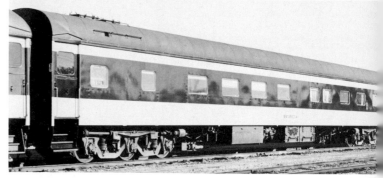

STANDARD ERA MATAPEDIA, thoroughly renovated to streamlined modernity though retaining its 8 section, drawing room, 2 compartment accommodations. CN's thoughtfulness included gold drapes, in addition to conventional shades in the rooms. The car was photographed in Churchill service in June, 1969.

Jim Scribbins

ONE OF THE more luxurious cars acquired by CN from U.S. roads is Kings Cove, which had been New York Central's Imperial Temple when the Road of the Century first acquired streamlined sleeping cars. It is of the 4 bedroom, 4 compartment (with upper berth windows) and 2 drawing room configuration; photographed in Winnipeg in April, 1964.

Jim Scribbins

SLEEPING CAR "GOLDEN SPIRE" was leased from the Rock Island for a period of time in the 1960's. The 8 roomette, 6 double bedroom sleeper once operated in the Golden State between Chicago and California. CN repainted the equipment leased from the Rock Island with black lettering. Note the CN at the left end of the car.

Canadian National

NECHAKO RIVER IS another example of a sleeping car purchased from US roads. This car is the former Erie Railroad's Charles Minot. It too is a 10-6 configuration.

Canadian National

CN ALSO OPERATED combination sleeper lounge cars, such as the Cape Chignecto shown here on the International Limited in Chicago in 1964. This equipment contained 2 double bedrooms and 2 compartments and a lounge section. While most of CN sleeping cars were railway operated, a number were leased to the Pullman Company. Such is the case with this car. Note the sub-lettering Pullman in the corners.

Jim Scribbins

OPEN OBSERVATION CARS were rail travelers' biggest delight before the advent of the dome car. Both CN and CP operated such equipment well into the 1950's on the transcontinental trains through the Rockies. Here we see the 15099 carrying the markers at Boston Bar, British Columbia about halfway through the Fraser Canyon.

Stan F. Styles

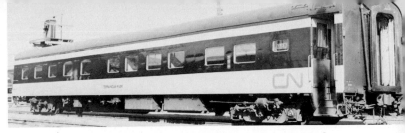

CN "TERRA NOVA RIVER" (No. 2130) is a 10 roomette, 6 double bedroom sleeper purchased from the Florida East Coast Railroad (the ex-Guatemala) in 1967.

Stan F. Styles

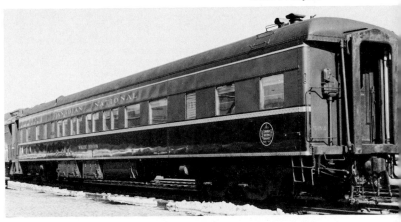

CN OPERATED A NUMBER of combination sleeper cafe or dining cars for trains that were assigned but one first class car in their consist. Such a car was White Brook (and other White cars), which was an 8 section 1 double bedroom cafe car. This car was built in 1939 by Canadian Car & Foundry, and streamlined versions arrived in the mid-1950's with the big car order. As of 1973, this car was still in service.

Jim Scribbins

DURING EQUIPMENT SHORTAGES, CN also leased sleeper lounges (as well as the sleepers previously mentioned). One such car was Great Northern's Winnipeg Club, an 8 duplex roomette, 2 double bedroom buffet lounge. This car was a natural because it served in international service on the GN's Winnipeg Limited, and all wording in the interior was in both French and English. The car had served on the Winnipeg Limited until replaced by a coach-dinette. Interestingly enough, the Winnipeg Limited operated over CN trackage between Noyes, Minnesota and Winnipeg, Manitoba.

Canadian National

FORT LAWRENCE WAS a four double bedroom, buffet lounge car with an enclosed observation room. The "Fort" series equipment had been rebuilt from open platform observation lounge sleeping cars in 1948.

Canadian National

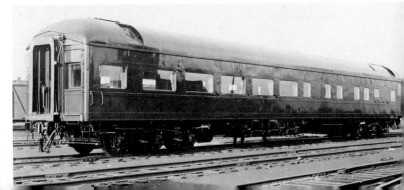

MANY OF THE "Fort" series cars were rebuilt a second time, this time as complete lounge cars during the year 1963. The Avant Garde is an example of such double rebuilding. In 1963, the car was remodeled from the Fort QuAppelle with the greater portion of the car being used in bar service. By 1969 the use of this equipment spread to the Churchill train on which Avant Garde is pictured at Thompson, Manitoba.

Jim Scribbins

WHAT UNDOUBTEDLY WERE the World's finest observation cars ever built, the eight double bedroom Skyview-lounge cars, originally trailed the Olympian Hiawatha over the Cascades and other scenic delights of the Milwaukee Road. The Gaspe is pictured here in its intended service on the Ocean at Truro, Nova Scotia in the Fall of 1966. When first on CN, these distinctive cars graced the Ocean and Scotian on their Montreal-Halifax journies. Later they were used in a variety of services: on seasonal trains between Winnipeg and Japser, in Summer on the Jasper-Prince Rupert trains, between Montreal and the Gaspe Peninsula on the Chaleur; and even on the Afternoon Rapido. At the time of this writing they stand out of service.

Jim Scribbins

TWO OF THE MOST unusual cars constructed in recent times were the Burrard and the Bedford. They were the last two open platform cars built for revenue service and contain seven double bedrooms, kitchen and lounge room. The cars are operated for special parties. At one time, the equipment operated in special executive club car service on the Afternoon Rapidos.

Canadian National

FINALLY CN's "PACIFIC," an open end observation car with 6 compartments, still carries the olive green color scheme. The car is used for historical purposes, and it is fitted with a diaphragm for mid-train operation.

Canadian National

DURING THE SECOND rebuilding, the cars were renamed with French names. This photo shows the interior of the Joie de Vivre, one of the twice upgraded standard era sleeper observations. This portion of the car was often referred to by CN as the "living room lounge." An example of the interior decor included red carpeting, modern furniture, wood paneled walls and a fluorescent ceiling. Some of the other French names included Bon Vivant, Matinee and Bon Voyage. This photo was taken by Jim Scribbins on a trip across Western Canada on the Super Continental in April, 1964.

IN MILWAUKEE ROAD SERVICE the Skytop Lounges were most noted for a circular couch type seat following the contour of the windows. CN changed them into small oases' containing swivel chairs and circular tables always adorned with bowls of pretzels.

Jim Scribbins

AGAINST THE FORWARD bulkhead of the Skyview lounges was a service bar. The ceiling contained the same attractive recessed flourescent lighting as did the upgraded full length lounges. The interior photos are of the car Fundy. The Skyviews were named after bays in Eastern Canada.

Jim Scribbins

USUALLY OFFICE OR Business cars do not operate in revenue service, their basic function providing rail officials with traveling offices for supervision and inspection of the railway. Few if any joy rides take place in such equipment because a trip out on the line means time away from the family and often long hours of hard work. They often serve as temporary headquarters out on the line when trouble arises. This photo shows the 95 at Calgary in September, 1974.

Stan F. Styles

CHAPTER 3

The Super Continental

The leader of the Canadian National passenger train fleet has been the Super Continental since April 24, 1955. She is a streamliner, and over part of the route she adds a dome car. She is a long train and often runs in the 20 car category. Christmas Holidays expand the train to consists that have not been seen in the United States since World War II, and during the summer there are four daily Super Continentals (trains 1 and 2, 3 and 4). The train offers the greatest variety of accomodations to be found on any train in North America, including CN's "Auto With You" plan each summer from Toronto to Edmonton and return on trains 3 and 4. All of these things add up to the Super Continental being one of the more superb trains not only in Canada, but all of North America.

Equipment for the Super is drawn from the 359 passenger cars (described in Chapter 2) that the Canadian National purchased in 1954. In addition, a number of existing cars were refurbished both inside and out to match the new streamlined cars in both comfort and decor. The 1955 Super Continental made an extremely fine looking train with its gold, green and black color scheme punctuated by CN's Maple Leaf in red, black and gold.

Canadian National developed a special motive power pool for the Super Continental. Eighteen locomotive sets were assigned for the two trains which operated in the following fashion: The cycle would begin by running west on trains No. 1 (Super Continental) from Montreal to Vancouver. The same engine would return on No. 4 (Continental) to Montreal and go west again on No. 3. Returning on No. 2 from Vancouver, the locomotive would run as far east as Capreol (the junction point for the Toronto and Montreal sections of the Super Continental) and then take train No. 52 to Toronto. the next trip would be on No. 53 to Capreol and return to Toronto on No. 54. Again she would go north on train No. 51 to Capreol, and then turn east ward on train No. 2 to Montreal. Upon arrival with 2, she would begin the cycle all over again the next day on train No. 1. The entire cycle would take 17 days. There was, however, a small twist in the diesel pool at that time. The CNR also operated a Montreal — Halifax cycle on four trains (2, 59, 60 and 1 in that order) and diesel units were interchangeable between the two pools. Consequently one or more units arriving at Montreal on train No. 4 might not go west on No. 3 but instead go east on No. 2 to Halifax.

The Super Continental made the transcontinental trip in substantially less time than the Continental. The 1955 schedule was 73 hours, 20 minutes; a reduction of 14 hours, 5 minutes for the Montreal — Vancouver run. This was more than a 16% reduction from the 87 hours, 25 minutes required by the Continental. East bound times were not as fast as the westbound runs. The time reductions were 10 hours, 25 minutes from Vancouver to Montreal and 10 hours, 30 minutes for the Toronto run. Eastbound running times were 72 hours, 5 minutes to Montreal and 69 hours to Toronto.

Setting up the faster schedules posed some interesting problems for CN. It was important for the Super to reach intermediate terminals, such as Winnipeg, Edmonton, Saskatoon and Jasper at convenient times plus sending the trains through the more scenic parts of their journeys in daylight hours. CN finally solved the problem by anchoring the schedule on Saskatoon and then built up east and west of there. The result was that the Super in both directions passed major cities and tourist resorts at times which were in some cases more convenient than those of the Continental. CN was unable to send No. 1 by Mount Robson, west of Jasper, in daylight hours but the present schedule of No. 3 passes Mt. Robson in daylight during the summer operation. However passengers were compensated by getting for the first time a daylight trip through the scenic canyon of the Fraser River east of Vancouver. Fortunately connecting schedules did not give CN major problems, although some adjustments were made at Toronto.

TRAIN NO. 52, the Toronto section of the Super Continental, passes South Parry, Ontario en route to Toronto after its long journey from Vancouver. This photo shows the original color scheme of the Super Continental, the handsome green, black and yellow with the maple leaf not only on the nose of the 6511, but also on each and every one of the passenger cars. The scenery is typical of Central Ontario.

Canadian National

The trains made connections at both Toronto and Montreal with trains to New York, Halifax and other points.

A substantial part of the overall time savings on the new schedule was achieved through shorter stops, particularly at major division points. Waiting time at Winnipeg was 25 minutes instead of 55 minutes. Stops at Saskatoon and Edmonton were 10 and 15 minutes respectively as against 25 to 40 minutes for the older schedule. Jasper was cut from 30 minutes to 10. The maximum speed limits were not raised, which in many cases are still 80 miles per hour.

Prior to and after the Super Continental went into operation, the CN concentrated on advertising in Canadian magazines and newspapers plus some radio and television spots. The emphasis was on the new train's more convenient arrival and departure times rather than on its faster schedule. Some extra money was allocated for magazine advertising in the United States. In that country the emphasis was on destinations served and equipment provided rather than on the new train as such. Canadian National's publicity also pointed out the availability of complete meals for $1.25 or less in the dinette and grill cars. This type of meal service increased overall dining car revenues as well as reducing costs.

Before going into service, the Super was opened to the press in Winnipeg, Saskatoon, Edmonton and Vancouver; and was displayed to the public at Montreal, Ottawa and Toronto. Special press runs were also made from Montreal, Ottawa and Toronto on April 23rd. In addition the CN made intensive use of special display and direct sales material such as posters counter cards, booklets of various types, special mailing pieces and time tables. Most were printed in English and French, but a number were printed in Spanish for Latin America and other languages for distribution in Europe.

To climax the publicity program, the CNR scheduled a special inaugural ceremony for the Super Continental. "Send-offs" were held at Montreal, Toronto and Vancouver for April 23rd, one day ahead of the train's actual departure. At Toronto the train was christened by the twin daughters of a railroad employee who were born on the Continental. At Vancouver, the train was christened by the wife of the mayor and at Montreal by a daughter of a train crew member. The CNR's pipe band and the color patrol of the CNR's Vimy branch of the Canadian Legion took part in the ceremonies. "Miss Super Continentals"—CNR employees—rode the first train west carrying tokens and greetings from the mayors of

48

Montreal, Ottawa and Toronto to the mayors of other cities along the route. They brought back tokens from the western cities in exchange.

The Canadian National did not expect its new train to be competitive with air service for transcontinental traffic from the standpoint of speed alone. Actually, through transcontinental business from Montreal or Toronto to Vancouver constituted only a relatively small portion of the traffic on the Continental. The CNR felt that the new train's speed, comfort and luxury would enable them to retain and enlarge the proportion of transcontinental business. They were correct. In addition the Super Continental continued to handle, as did the earlier Continental, a substantial volume of on and off, point to point business, such as Montreal to Winnipeg, Winnipeg to Saskatoon, Edmonton to Vancouver and other points. As the train went into operation, the Canadian National watched traffic results with care and interest. A substantial amount of research went into the train to determine how the public used it, what the public wanted and what the public would pay for. Consequently, there have been a number of changes over the years.

The very first planned consist for the Super was as follows:

1 Express Car
1 Baggage Car
2 Coaches
3 Tourist Sleeping Cars

1 Dinette Car/Montreal-Winnipeg
1 Tourist-Coffee Shop Car, Winnipeg-Vancouver
1 Dining Car, Toronto-Vancouver
1 Lounge Car
2 or more Sleeping Cars, depending upon the season.

The above list of equipment shows the train west of Capreol. This equipment consist was also the basic consist of the train with additional equipment added during summer and the Christmas holidays. However, by October, 1959 the basic consist had changed somewhat as follows:

2 or more Express and Baggage Cars All points
1 Coach Montreal-Vancouver
1 Coach Montreal-Ottawa
1 Coach Toronto-Vancouver
1 Dining Car Toronto-Vancouver
1 Diner-Lounge Montreal-Capreol
1 Coffee Shop Toronto-Capreol
1 Coffee Shop Lounge Montreal-Vancouver
1 Parlor Car Montreal-Ottawa
1 Tourist Roomette Slpr. Montreal-Edmonton
1 Tourist Roomette Slpr. Toronto-Vancouver
1 1 4 DBR Buffet Lounge Toronto-Vancouver

FREIGHT UNIT 9122 and passenger unit 6501 lead train No. 2, the eastbound Super Continental east of Jasper, Alberta on August 2, 1956. This photo shows the differences in the freight and passenger color schemes.

George-Paterson Collection

1   4 Sec., 8 Dup Rmt., 4 DBR Toronto-Vancouver
1   4 Sec., 8 Dup Rmt., 4 DBR Montreal-Vancouver
1   4 Sec., 8 Dup Rmt., 4 DBR Winnipeg-Saskatoon

The total number of cars west of Capreol was eleven or more for the basic consist.

The scheduled running time of train 1 and 2 was substantially speeded up by the fall of 1959 too. The original 73 hour, 20 minute schedule was cut to 69 hours, 45 minutes on the Montreal to Vancouver run. East bound running times were cut two hours from 72 hours, 5 minutes to 70 hours, 5 minutes.

The most significant development of the first five years was the change in Tourist accommodations. The open section car was discontinued in favor of the new Tourist Roomette. Further the roomettes were available for holders of coach tickets, and up to 1959 were the most luxurious accommodations offered for coach class passengers. 24 Duplex Roomette sleepers were assigned to trains 1 and 2 for the Tourist service. Regular 14 Section-Kitchen Tourist Sleeprs were still available on the Super's running mate, the secondary Continental

Tourist sleeping car passengers also had access to a special tourist lounge section.

Summer time consists, as we reported before, were huge and still are. During the summer of 1964, the Super Continental was running with the following consist west of Capreol:

2   or more express, baggage and dormitory cars
3   Coaches
1   Coach Lounge Car
1   Dinette
4   Sleeping Cars (4-4-2, 12-1, 24 Rmt., and 4-8-4)
2   Dining Cars
1   Club Lounge Car
3   Sleeping Cars (4-8-4, 22 Rmt., and 12-1)

A grand total of 17 cars as compared to the 11 or so during the off season.

There were some more major differences by the summer of 1964. Tourist accommodations had been discontinued, but the reader will note that 12 section, 1 drawing room sleepers were still being run on the Super Continental. No other *major* train in North America (with the exception of Mexico) had 12-1 sleepers still included in the consist.

1964 is a significant year for the Canadian National's passenger service. On May 24th the Railway added a new transcontinental train, the Panorama. The new train ran on a complementary schedule to the Super Continental, while the old Continental lost its name and became a Montreal, Toronto and Saskatoon schedule. The Panorama offered the same types of services as the Super such as, hospitality hours, games times for young and

ALL AIR TRAVEL, as well as highway, is delayed as a snow storm sweeps up the St. Lawrence River valley. However, the Montreal section of the Super departs Montreal en route to Vancouver with a full crowd and on time.
Canadian National

THE WESTBOUND SUPER Continental, train No. 1, crosses the bridge at Sioux Lookout, Ontario en route to Vancouver.

Canadian National

old and all of the accommodations offered by the fleet leader. In addition the classic Red, White and Blue fares were being offered coast to coast.

Although the tourist accommodations had been discontinued, the service would be resumed under a new name in 1965.

The year 1964 is also significant for one other reason. During that year the CN purchased six Super Dome lounge cars from the Milwaukee Road, and placed the refurbished cars in service on the Super Continental and Panorama. Dubbed Sceneramic Lounge cars, they operated westbound from Jasper to Vancouver and eastbound from Vancouver to Edmonton. They operated in the reverse fashion on the Panorama. and thus the Canadian National completed 1964 with twin transcontinental streamliner service including dome lounge cars through the Canadian Rockies in daylight.

1965 brought still more changes to the Super Continental. Business was expanding and effective with the June 23, 1965 schedule change, the Super Continental ran as two spearate trains from Montreal and Toronto and Vancouver. Trains 51

and 52, normally operated only between Toronto and Capreol began through service to the west coast on the above date. Trains 1 and 2 continued to run in the normal fashion. With such a schedule, Canadians had a choice of three trains each way daily between the East and the Pacific Coast. In 1965, only the Santa Fe and Union Pacific railroads ran more transcontinental train service. Trains 51 and 52 ran until September 8th of that year.

With the expanded summer service, equipment took on a new twist. With the exception of the Jasper-Vancouver Sceneramic Lounge car (both directions) and a 17 Roomette Winnipeg-Saskatoon sleeper, the entire consist of trains 1 and 2 operated between Montreal and Vancouver. During the summer season of 1965, the CNR did not operate any Montreal-Ottawa set out parlor cars and coaches as was customary during lighter traffic periods of the year. In addition to an express, baggage and dormitory car and the two previously mentioned cars, trains 1 and 2 carried two 14 Section "Dormette" sleepers, one coach lounge car, one reserved seat coach, one cafeteria car,

51

THE EASTBOUND SUPER Continental shares the Jasper station with train No. 10, which arrived from Prince Rupert before the arrival of No. 2. Note the heavy consist of head-end equipment on No. 10, which travels through a very remote area of Canada. The consist of No. 2 is a whopping 18 cars including an express refer painted in the streamlined color scheme.

three streamlined sleepers (22 Rmt.; two 4 sec., 8 Rmt., 4 DBR), one diner, one club lounge car, 2 standard sleepers (12-1, 8-2-1) and one more streamlined sleeper (4 DBR, 4 Comp., 2 DR) for a total of 14 cars west of Jasper not including head-end equipment.

Trains 51 and 52, with the exception of the Scenoramic Lounge between Jasper and Vancouver, operated their entire consist between Toronto and Vancouver. This included two 14 section "Dormette" sleepers, one coach lounge, one reserved seat coach, one cafeteria car, three streamlined sleepers (24 roomettes, two 4 sec.; 8 Rmt., 4 DBR cars), one diner, one club lounge and finally three more sleepers (8-2-1; 5 Comp., 3 DR and 12-1) for total of 15 cars west of Jasper not including head-end equipment.

Altogether the passenger had a selection of reclining coach seats, sections, duplex roomettes, roomettes, double bedrooms, compartments, drawing rooms and a new accomodation called the "Dormette." Dormette sections were sold in open section sleeping cars at a rate lower than standard upper and lower berths or sections. (A full section includes both the upper and lower berth and the passenger has a choice of purchasing either the upper or lower or the complete section.) The dormette actually signaled the return of tourist sleeping car service, but under a new name and with a slightly different pricing arrangement. Furthermore the new rate system was actually less expensive than the old tourist car rates five years previous to 1965. Although fares were lower, the CN did not downgrade the service which remained at the same or higher standards of previous tourist car upper and lower berth service on the Super Continental.

In the fall of 1965, CN resumed the standard operating procedures of the Super including the combining of the Montreal and Toronto sections at Capreol and the Ottawa set out parlor car service.

The summer of 1966 found the Super again running separately from Montreal and Toronto to the west coast in addition to the Panorama. The same heavy consists of the summer of 1965 were again the rule of thumb. The Toronto train numbers were changed from 51 and 52 to 3 and 4, and they have not been changed since that time.

1967 brought Expo 67 and was the biggest year yet for the Super. Consists were incredibly large and the separate sections began running earlier (June 1st) and ran later (September 30th) than in previous years. The consist of 1 and 2 included 9 sleepers, two coaches, one coach lounge, one cafeteria car, two diners and one club lounge plus the dome lounge from Edmonton to Vancouver.

THE SUPER CONTINENTAL crosses some of the most beautiful mountain ranges in the World in Western Canada. CN also equips motive power with portable headlights to assist engineers in seeing around curves. Note the two extra lamps at the bottom of the C and N.

Canadian National

West of Edmonton, 1 and 2 carried an additional coach for a grand total of 17 cars not including head-end equipment, which was usually two or three cars. Trains 3 and 4 carried virtually an identical consist of 17 passenger cars not including head-end equipment. The Panorama was equally heavy. Again in the fall, the Super was reduced in size and included an Ottawa set out parlor, coaches and diner lounge.

The Fall 1967 Super included two 12 sections, 1 drawing room sleepers in its consist of 6 transcontinental sleepers between Vancouver and Montreal. The name of the drawing room was changed to "Family Room." There were two thru coaches plus two diners and a club lounge car for a total of 11 cars excluding head-end traffic. The dome car did not run on 1 and 2 that fall and winter.

1968 followed the typical pattern of previous years with the Super running in separate Montreal and Toronto sections to Vancouver during the heavy summer period. Both trains again drew heavy consists but ran only from June 14th to September 14th, which was a somewhat shorter period of time than in 1967. Again the consist were solid Montreal-Vancouver without the Ottawa set outs. The dome lounge cars ran only between Edmonton and Vancouver.

1969 marked another dramatic change in the Super Continental. During that summer period she did not run in separate sections. However, CN did operate a nameless train, numbers 7 and 8, three days a week between Montreal, Toronto and Jasper, and the Panorama operated between Winnipeg and Vancouver. The Super, meanwhile, became an even heavier train and included four Ottawa set out cars. West of Capreol the train consisted of one coach lounge car, three coaches, two 24 duplex roomette sleeper "Dormettes" (which was the first summer the duplex roomette cars ran in dormette service), seven sleeping cars, one club lounge car and two dining cars. This did not include the two to three head-end cars and the dome lounge (Edmonton-Vancouver), one more coach (Saskatoon-Jasper) and one more sleeper (Winnipeg-Saskatoon). The minimum number of cars was 18 west of Capreol and was frequently over 20. The fall, 1969 time table showed the Super with but 11 cars west of Capreol with additional cars on the Montreal-Ottawa run, one sleeper between Winnipeg and Saskatoon and the dome lounge on the Edmonton-Vancouver circuit.

1969 however was the only year that the Super Continental did not run in separate Toronto and Montreal sections. Effective with January 7, 1970, the Panorama disappeared from the time tables

53

TRAIN NO. 2 PAUSES at Sioux Lookout, Ontario as the red jacketed Porter inspects the platform. The window air conditioners on the depot indicate that the summer days can be as hot as winter nights are cold. The individualistically styled windows of the 10-6 sleeper Vermillion River betray the ancestry of the car as Milwaukee Road's Lake Pepin. The photo was taken in September, 1971.

Jim Scribbins

SOME STREAMLINED COACHES during the "passenger offensive" of the mid-1960's had their smoking sections redone as an attractive beverage section, with drinks prepared in an adjacent service area and the ever present pretzels on the tables. The photo is the interior of coach lounge car No. 3006 in service on the Super Continental in April, 1964.

Jim Scribbins

after having been slowly cut down until it was but a Winnipeg-Vancouver train. From 1970 through 1975, the Super Continental has run a cycle of combined sections during the fall, winter and spring; and separate sections during the summer months. The train continues to offer a wide variety of accommodations, which has been a tradition ever since 1955.

In fact, Super Continental services are now even more varied than they were in 1955. Accommodations include the *Dayniter*, which is a luxury coach service at a slight premium with adjustable reclining deep cushioned seats with padded leg rests and plenty of leg room. In addition, dayniter cars are fully carpeted, contain decorative fabric wall coverings, acoustic soundproofing and numerous other features. Sleeping accommodations include roomettes, duplex roomettes, double bedrooms, standard mini-bedrooms and standard upper and lower berths. In addition there is a coach lounge service for all coach passengers, cafe lounge car service, club lounge car service, dining car and the dome lounge car through the Rockies. The latter operates from Winnipeg during single train operation and between Edmonton and Vancouver during the two section service.

In 1972, CN began an "Auto With You" plan between Toronto and Edmonton on the Toronto section of the Super. The new service, offered only during the summer is a variation of CN's regular Car-Go-Rail service but enables passengers to take their autos along on the same train. Prior to 1975,

it was Canada's only auto-train service such as found in the United States to and from Florida. As with Auto-Train, Canadian passengers making use of the "Auto-With-You" plan must travel on the same train and make advance reservations. The automobiles are transported in a special enclosed auto transporter attached to the rear of the Super. At the present time, two-wheeled tent trailers are accepted under this plan.

Passengers must pay a one charge of around $225 for the transportation of the auto plus a minimum of two regular adult coach fares according to the day on which travel commences (red, white or blue days). For round trip travel the cost is double the one way fare. Sleeping car accommodations carry an additional cost. Passengers receive their automobiles soon after arrival at either Edmonton or Toronto. Consideration was being given in 1975 to expanding the service to Vancouver. Car-Go-Rail, of course, offers fast freighting of your automobile between Halifax, Moncton, Montreal, Toronto, Winnipeg, Saskatoon, Edmonton and Vancouver, as well as Ottawa westward.

The Super Continental has now been running for over twenty years. She is now basking in the midst of an energy crunch; she has changed her image from green, black and gold to black, white and orange. She has become part of Canada and represents Canada. She is still the flag bearer for the Canadian National passenger fleet. The Super Continental is indeed a "Super" train and Canadians everywhere can be proud of her.

THE INTERIOR OF the former Milwaukee Road dome lounge cars have been modified extensively by Canadian National. Much of the former coach type seats have been replaced with easy chairs, sofa and table seating for more extensive club lounge service. Interior colors are varied and the new arrangement is very restful and attractive.

Canadian National

AT THE PRESENT time (February, 1975), the only equal to the Dayniter coaches are Auto-Train's coaches on their Florida runs. CN equipment is decorated in soft restful colors with leg rest seats, individual tables for each passenger, drapes on the windows, carpeting, individual reading lamps for each seat (spot light fixtures in the baggage racks) and can be classified as the most luxurious economy train travel.

Canadian National

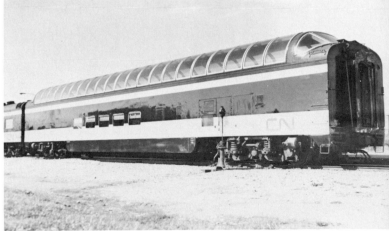

DAYNITER COACHES HAVE BEEN and are being rebuilt from coaches in the 5437 and 5654 series. This equipment is the ultimate in deluxe coach train travel, and is part of the accommodations offered on the Super Continental. The 5700 was photographed in Vancouver in September, 1974 by Stan F. Styles.

SCENERAMIC DOME LOUNGE CARS are assigned to the Super Continental through the Canadian Rockies. The Fraser is shown here at Vancouver after purchase from the Milwaukee Road in 1965.

Stan F. Styles

ALTHOUGH THERE ARE tentative plans for expansion, the "Auto-With-You" plan presently operates during the summers between Toronto and Edmonton. The cars are loaded into enclosed cars idential to the Auto-Train equipment. Indeed, Auto-Train purchased their auto-carriers from CN. It is a travel innovation that bears watching as it has been highly successful for Auto-Train and British Rail.

Canadian National

THE TORONTO SECTION of the Super Continental, trains 3 and 4, carries the "Auto-With-You" car between Toronto and Edmonton. Not equipped with steam lines, the car is attached to the rear of 3 and 4 which also makes it convenient for switch crews to pick up the car for unloading at Toronto and Edmonton.

Canadian National

THE RUNNING MATE to the Super Continental during the 1960's was the Panorama. Here we see train No. 6, the eastbound Panorama, crossing the Assiniboine River for an on time arrival at Winnipeg from Vancouver in June, 1969.

Jim Scribbins

CHAPTER 4

Commuter Train Service

Suburban train service was well organized by the time Canadian National came into existence in 1919. Indeed such service was widespread throughout much of the CN. In fact service was offered on the following six routes between 1919 and the Depression:

Montreal-St. Rosalie	38.4 miles
Montreal-Vaudreuil	25.5 miles
Montreal-St. Eustache sur le Lac	17.0 miles
Toronto-Hamilton	38.7 miles
Winnipeg-Transcona	7.1 miles
Moncton-Pt. du Chene	19.1 miles

The frequency on all routes, except for the Moncton service, was not less than every two hours on the average and more frequent during rush hours. In some cases, service was hourly or oftener.

Commuter train service has never rated much excitement with anybody. The trains have been chronic money loosers, and railway managements world wide have taken it on the chin for not providing up to date modern service. Canadian National, with a few exceptions, has been in the same boat.

CN operated the various types of services with old green coaches with straight back seats. In the early 1920's, every coach was a wooden car and many were open enders.

All routes were powered by steam with two exceptions. The Winnipeg-Transcona line which was operated by gas-electric motor cars, and the Montreal-St. Eustache sur le Lac line which was electrified when first opened. The name of St. Eustache sur le Lac was eventually changed to Deux Montagnes. In addition, there is a short branch from Val Royal to Cartierville (0.9 miles) which is also electrified.

With the exception of the Hamilton and the Deux Montagnes services, all of the above listed routes have slowly disappeared over the years. The automobile and the depression are responsible for the abandonment of this train service.

In addition to the heavy Deux Montagnes service, CN once operated a frequent train service to Vaudreuil in the Montreal area. This particular route was built in the 1850's by the Grand Trunk. It was the first rail route that went through the west end of Montreal and followed the shore of Lake St. Louis. This route continues to Toronto and is now part of the Montreal-Toronto main line. Suburban traffic began almost immediately although it was very small. The villages were rural and few people had any reason to travel to Montreal regularly. However by the 1870's, some of the villages such as Dorval, Pointe Claire, Ste. Annes and Vaudreuil were growing and the Grand Trunk put on trains that stopped at these and other locations. The result was that more people moved into the area and by the 1880's a complete suburban service was blossoming. Traffic grew substantially for the next three decades, and the railway invested in open end suburban cars and a small fleet of tank engines for suburban train power. The Vaudreuil line supported about 50 commuter trains daily in 1926 (about 25 in each direction). However this number began to diminish with declining traffic. The service was cut back to Dorval in 1955 and discontinued entirely in 1961. This left the Canadian Pacific Railway has the only suburban service along the Lakeshore Route west of Montreal.

There are some interesting stories concerning the competition between the CPR and CNR along the route. With trains running about the same times, and stopping at the same towns, the trains of the two companies often raced. Sometimes, it has been said, commuters barely had time to detrain or to board when the race was close. Having spent many miles on commuter trains, this writer is sure that such antics on the part of the train crews did nothing to endear the CPR or the CNR to the suburbanites along the Lakeshore Route.

The Deux Montagnes line is now the most important of any Montreal commuter train services. And as of 1974, this route is the only heavy-duty electrified line in Canada, although it is not the only electric operation. The Montreal line is operated with 2400 volts direct current. The electrified

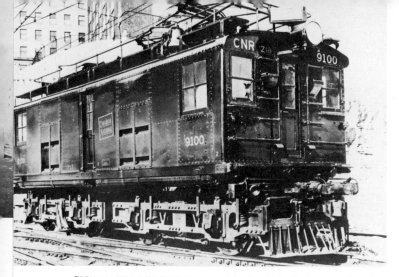

CN 9100 WAS ELEVEN years old when this photo was taken in the Montreal Terminals in 1925. These electrics were built by General Electric in 1914 and many are still in service as of 1975.

Harold K. Vollrath Collection

COACH 4959 IS PART of the high capacity standard coach fleet that makes up a majority of the commuter car equipment. This equipment can carry from 154 to 205 passengers including standees. Although this photo shows a standard coach in green and black, all commuter equipment has been repainted white and black with a red-orange CN.

Canadian National

few Canadians knew it—and literally no one in the USA took the project seriously enough to consider implementation of the basic philosophy and operating procedures in similar situations.

The next step was for the Government to place the responsibility for implementation and administration of the new commuter service with the Ontario Department of Highways. A Commuter Service Department was set up by Canadian National to plan and coordinate the railway's participation in the project and to handle its daily operations. As 1965 progressed, the distinctive GO Transit logo (a stylized G and O in bright green linked together by the white horizontal bars of the letter T lying on its side) was designed by the visual redesign staff of Candian National. Furthermore, other developmental work included station locations and property acquisition, railway construction engineering, scheduling and consists, maintenance requirements, crew arrangements, labor negotiations, fare structure and ticketing, public promotion and actual operations of trains. The kick off date for the new service was May 23, 1967, just 24 months after the announcement to proceed came in May, 1965.

The initial equipment purchased in 1966 and 1967 consisted of eight diesel locomotives, 40 coaches and nine self-propelled cars for a total cost of $8 million. The total initial capital cost of GO Transit for both plant and equipment was close to $24 million. The reader should compare this figure with the highway construction costs noted earlier in this section. Top speed of the special GP-40's built by General Motors is 83 miles per hour, and can accelerate a fully loaded 10 car train from a standing start to 60 mph in 2.3 minutes in a distance of 1.5 miles.

Hawker Siddeley Canada Limited produced the coaches and self propelled cars at the Thunder Bay, Ontario plant. The cars were constructed ex-

THIS PHOTO SHOWS the interior of high capacity coach No. 4916. Note the hand railings for standees and the advertising posters at locations where standees will have a chance to look at them. Baggage racks are placed over the flip over seats.

Canadian National

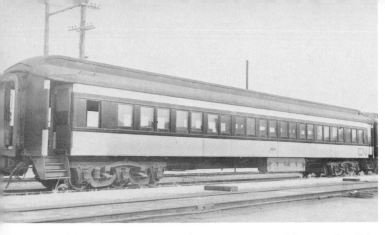

COACH 6600 WAS A high capacity car with room for 188 passengers including standees. There were but ten cars in this series from 6600 to 6609 built in 1923. The 6600 is shown here prior to conversion to a work car in September, 1974 at Calgary.
Stan F. Styles

MULTIPLE-UNIT ELECTRIC coaches are operated with one power or motor unit with two trailers. Here a six car train scoots along through the Roxboro Area near Montreal.
Canadian National

tensively of aluminum, which achieved a 40% reduction in weight for the coaches, and a 20% reduction for the self-propelled cars. This was accomplished without the sacrifice of capacity and safety, and has resulted in a savings in operating and maintenance costs for both the equipment and track structure.

GO Transit also uses the Push-Pull concept pioneered by the Chicago & North Western Railway in Chicago in 1960. Eight of the coaches are equipped with remote control operating cabs which eliminate the time consuming necessity to run the locomotives around the train at terminal stations.

The self propelled cars are of two different types. Two of the coaches have control cabs at both

A PAIR OF English electrics power a commuter train near the Monkland Station. Note the street crossing flashers with both English and French.
Canadian National

ends, while the seven others are equipped with controls at one end only. All are operated in pairs or multiple sets, which are especially suited to off peak requirements. However they can be combined into longer train sets to supplement locomotive hauled trains during rush hours. Each self propelled car is equipped with a 330 horsepower Rolls Royce engine and has a top speed of 80 miles per hour.

Exterior surfaces of both types of coaches are brushed aluminum with white ends, a white trim along the side and the green GO Transit symbol. Eleven large scenic view windows are spaced along each wall. Double-width folding doors at both ends of each car may be remote controlled from any point in the train.

Coaches are carried on four wheel inboard-bearing trucks equipped with brake equipment incorporating a proportioning feature which maintains a constant deceleration rate regardless of differences in the passenger load.

All GO trains are equipped with two-way radio communication with train dispatchers, the commuter administration center, and the maintenance department. Further all GO Transit coaches feature a versatile on-train communication system providing private inter-crew communications, announcements to passenger areas and a means for addressing platform crowds through externally mounted speakers on both sides of one end of each car.

Since 1967, the equipment roster has grown substantially. In 1968 14 coaches were purchased. A further 30 coaches were added in 1973/74 and a further order of 30 was placed recently for delivery in the fall of 1975.

61

ONE OF THE ORIGINAL GP-40's with a westbound GO train near Markham Road in east end Toronto. CN's Point St. Charles Shops in Montreal are modifying the original geeps with new sound muffling components that reduce the noise level of the power generators by nearly 80%. The 9805 received the new green and white scheme in January, 1975.
Government of Ontario Transit

The year 1974 also saw seven more locomotives join the roster in two orders, one of four and a later one of three. These are conventional GP-40-2 GMD models without auxiliary power generators, which make them different from the original eight GP-40's. The new units require an Auxiliary Power Control Unit to be part of the consist of the train.

These Auxiliary Power Control Units were designed and built from Ontario Northland FP-7A's. The five APCU's contain a diesel motor-alternator set to provide electrical power to the train. The APCU's are incapable of independent movement and they provide both the function of the auxiliary generator found on the original GO locomotives and the function of the cab cars.

A great deal of consideration was given to the decor and interior appointments of the coaches to lure the motorist away from his automobile. The predominant wall color throughout is beige-gray complemented by green on the vestibule bulkheads and rosewood and ebony on compartment bulkheads. The flooring in the cars is actually a continuous rubber installation. As of January, 1975, GO is experimenting with carpeting in two coaches. If the carpeting works out well, it will be installed in the 30 car order due in late 1975. The ceilings consist of white translucent plastic panels which are lit up concealed fluorescent units to highlight the bright interior appearance and provide glarefree night illumination.

The coaches are divided into two passenger compartments, one of which contains 40 seats for smokers and the other 54 for non-smokers in the traditional Canadian coach arrangement. The bucket type seats are non-rotating, most of which are grouped in facing pairs to achieve a sense of roominess. Variety is afforded by wall mounted seat groups at three locations in each coach.

The original territory served extended from Hamilton to Pickering with Toronto approximately in the middle of the 60 mile route. Eleven of the 15 stations along the route were newly constructed for commuters. Spaced from two to seven miles apart, the stations are located close to major arteries to provide easy access for the majority of people within their defined catchment areas. The new depots are totally different from the usual railway station which provides ticketing and waiting rooms in a single building. The new GO stations consist of a separate ticket office and several on-platform shelters a length of a car apart to distribute passengers. The entire depot and parking lots are well lit up at night. Toronto's Union Station was also renovated to provide facilities for GO passengers, and to keep them separate from inter-city passenger activities of Canadian National and Canadian Pacific.

Passenger convenience was one of the prime considerations in setting up the schedule for GO. It was stipulated that the trains must run far more often than just a rush hour service. Consequently, hourly service was developed with 20 minute headways for the rush hours. Also trains were scheduled through the Union Station instead of terminating there. Trains are scheduled from 6:00 AM until midnight between Oakville, Toronto and Pickering. Two additional trains operate to and from Hamilton during the rush hours each week day. On weekends only the basic hourly service between Oakville and Pickering prevails.

GO trains are allowed 37 minutes for the 21 mile run from Union Station to Oakville or Pickering for an average speed of 35 miles per hour. The run from Hamilton to Toronto consumes 64 minutes for the 39 mile trip. Each run stops for six minutes at Toronto to allow time for complete train loads to board or leave the train. Ten minute stops are allowed at each end of the line for crews to change ends. GO's push pull trains operate with the locomotives on the west end of the train with the cab controlled cars or APCU's on the east end.

When the service originally started, the locomotives were located on the east end of the trains. However, as a result and part of the noise abatement program at GO's Willowbrook maintenance facility, the locomotives have been relocated to the west end, thus placing them farther from neighborhood residences when they are idling at Willowbrook. Therefore, the cab cars and APCU's are now located at the east end.

Canadian National crews man GO trains and bid on the assignments as with any other CN train operation.

Prior to the new service, Canadian National laid 19 miles of new mainline track and five miles of sidings in the Port Credit, Clarkson and Scarborough-Guildwood areas. 100 new track switches were installed, many of which are high

ONE OF THE original GP-40's (actually designated GP-40TC for Toronto Commuter and with a CN road class of GFE-430a), awaits its first assignment at GO's Willowbrook maintenance facility on November 26, 1974 after having new muffling equipment installed to reduce noise levels of the power generator, and repainted in the new green and white scheme. The new colors are most attractive and eye catching.
GO Transit

THE BRIGHT INTERIORS of the GO coaches feature indirect lighting and large picture windows. This car is one of the 30 built in 1973-74 and features stanchions for the benefit of standee passengers.

GO Transit

THE EXTERIOR of the GO coaches boasts brushed aluminum sides and white painted steel ends. Since this picture was taken, the cars have been renumbered into the 9900 series.

GO Transit

speed crossovers, to allow trains to move from one track to another without a loss of time and with a minimum of interference with other trains. A centralized traffic control system replaced an automatic block signal system. Dispatchers at CN's Maple freight classification yard (18 miles northwest of downtown Toronto) control GO movements over the Oakville and Kingston Subdivisions along the Lakeshore.

GO's newest rail route to Georgetown was opened April 29, 1974. Operating with three trains each way five days a week, the Northwest route is now (January, 1975) carrying about 3,000 people daily and experiencing a steady growth. The GO service supplemented the one train each way a day to Guelph run by CN which was handling about 600 people a day. At the present time, the CN train is still operating under order of the Canadian Transport Commission but has shrunk to an average of two cars.

GO expects to open its third rail route from Toronto to Richmond Hill in early 1976. Once again operating over CN trackage, the service will initially consist of three trains each a day, five days a week.

Maintenance and equipment servicing is conducted at the Willowbrook maintenance yard. The yard is the former CN Mimico freight car repair center. The new trackage has been arranged to permit full servicing and running repairs to trains wherever they are parked in the yard. Each coach is cleaned both inside and out every day. Exterior washing is handled by CN's mechanical car washer at the Spadina Avenue coach yard. Train schedules are arranged so that equipment passes through the washer daily on the way into or out of service. GO diesel power is maintained at the Spadina Diesel shop by Canadian National shop crews.

The streamlined cars owned by GO Transit are not the only equipment operated in this commuter territory. Both locomotives and coaches owned by the Ontario Northland Railway have frequently been in service during the non-vacation time periods. During the summer of 1974, GO Transit tested out Canadian Pacific double deck passenger equipment. The bi-level equipment test was largely successful, but GO has not yet placed an order. However chances are that by the time this book is in print in the Fall of 1975, bi-level equipment will be on order. They will likely be much different from Canadian Pacific gallery cars.

GO Transit has also invested in buses and a coordinated service arrangement has been set up extending the territory served by GO Transit. This arrangement has proven very convenient for GO passengers.

Although GO Transit loses approximately $2 million annually, when one compares that figure with highway construction and maintenance costs it is obvious that the rail system of GO Transit is the most sensible way to go. Consequently careful planning is going on for the future. For example, it is thought that the Lakeshore service now in operation will be replaced with double deck cars for a 75% increase in capacity. GO Transit and Canadian Pacific are now working on plans to extend service to Streetsville and Milton from Toronto. This will be the first operation not on CN trackage. A Super GO is envisioned where additional trackage will be built on the Lakeshore Route with improved signal equipment to achieve exclusive use of two tracks by GO during rush hours. This would permit train operation at four minute inter-

A TWO CAR SCOOT of self-propelled GO cars provides off peak service. This train was photographed at Longbranch.

GO Transit

vals instead of the 20 minutes which is possible today on shared tracks. The Super GO concept also considers electrification of the service for added reliability and environmental factors.

The Lakeshore service now carries more than 20,000 passengers daily. With double deck equipment this could be increased to about 35,000. Super GO frequencies could reach 200,000.

GO Transit is one of the finest suburban train operations in the world. The schedules, equipment and future planning really speak for themselves. The Government of Ontario and Canadian National are to be congratulated for their recognition of the critical need for a balanced transportation system. Many communities and states in the USA could benefit greatly with a GO Transit concept.

In addition to the GO services, CN offers limited commuter service with one rush hour train each way between Toronto and Stouffville, 28.6 miles; Toronto and Barrie, 63.0 miles and Toronto and Guelph, 48.8 miles. These are essentially local

trains but they are scheduled in such a way to provide commuters train service to and from work.

Suburban service has had its ups and downs since 1919 when Canadian National was established. The former Grand Trunk Railway System also operated a suburban service out of Detroit and Chicago. The Chicago service died early, although it once extended all the way to Valparaiso, Indiana. The Detroit service still exists on the Grand Trunk Western Railroad.

It is always difficult to predict the future, but one thing is certain, the automobile cannot continue in the same fashion as the past 20 years. The train is the most economical form of passenger transportation, and it must be part of the development of a balanced transportation system. Again this writer would like to say that Canadian National is to be complemented for their part in providing commuter service in Montreal and Toronto, which has been the most frustrating part of the rail business and operations for decades.

GO SELF-PROPELLED cars can be operated with any number of cars in the consist in exactly the same manner as Rail Diesel Cars. The interiors of these coaches are the same as the locomotive hauled equipment.

GO Transit

A NEW GP-40-2 powers a westbound GO train through Bayview Junction en route to Hamilton, Ontario. The new geeps sport CN's crew comfort cabs and were the first to carry GO's new green and white paint scheme.

GO Transit

GO TRANSIT APCU No. 9861 leads an eastbound train through Bayview Junction near Hamilton, Ontario. Power on the opposite end is a new GP-40-2 delivered in 1974.

GO Transit

GO TRANSIT AUXILIARY Power Control Unit No. 9861 poses beside cab car 9853 at the Willowbrook maintenance facility in west end Toronto. the APCU's provide the same remote control point as the cab cars, but also contain a diesel power generator to provide electrical power for the GO cars. They were built using retired FP-7A locomotives from the Ontario Northland Railway, and are most attractive in their green and white color scheme. These units are used on trains powered by the new GP-40-2's. Further CN's Research and Development Department has been able to reduce the noise level of the power generators substantially.

GO Transit

One of the interesting things to note on Canadian National is that the numbering system is actually a symbol number. In most cases, especially on the main lines, most of the freights operate as extras. Yet on many subdivisions, the symbol freight may operate as a second or third class train. An example of this can be found on the Kinghorn Subdivision of the Lakehead Area between Longlac Junction and Thunder Bay North. Here symbol freights 307 and 308 (between Montreal and Winnipeg via Thunder Bay) operate as trains 921 and 922 respectively. However, as stated above most trains operate as extras so that dispatchers can have more flexibility in operating freight trains.

Of all the railroads in the US and Canada, CN takes top honors in the operation of mixed trains. A mixed train is a combination freight and passenger train, usually a local type of run. CN operates such trains in every province on all parts of the system except for southwestern Ontario. Normally such a local train operates with the freight cars on the head end with a baggage car and coach, or simply a combine bringing up the rear. It seems almost strange to think that mixed trains continue to operate in 1975 when they have virtually disappeared in the United States. However, there are a number of locations in Canada where road conditions are not the best. Further, since the railway is the only all weather transportation system, the mixed train is sometimes the only reliable form of transportation despite its slower speed. Furthermore, the mixed train still delivers such important items such as groceries, etc. to many of the outposts that are served only by Canadian National Railways.

This chapter barely does justice to the entire freight service operation of the Canadian National Railways. However it is hoped that it will provide the reader with some idea of the magnitude of the service provided by Canadian National. It must be remembered that without that freight service, the economies of the United States and Canada would not be as great as they are today.

A WESTBOUND WAY FREIGHT trundles across the Grand River bridge at Paris, Ontario on July 4, 1953 with 20 cars.
Elmer Treloar

EXTRA 6234 EAST ROLLS by the tower at Hamilton Junction en route to Eastern Canadian points with coal from the mines in Pennsylvania. A good deal of the consist of the train are Erie Railroad coal hoppers on this sunny July 4, 1953.

Elmer Treloar

A NORTHBOUND CN freight snakes around the reverse curves at Hamilton Junction, Ontario on July 26, 1953. One of the things that has impressed this writer about CN main lines is the high quality of track. Notice the neatness of the track materials stored at this location.

Elmer Treloar

CN NO. 7320, AN 0-6-0 type switcher, moves on to the turn table at Fort Frances, Ontario. She will soon resume her switching duties.

A. Robert Johnson

THE CREW OF Consolidation No. 2509 awaits the highball to continue east from Boston Bar, British Columbia as a track inspector on a hand propelled track car heads up the line.

Stan F. Styles

0-6-0 SWITCHER NO. 7304 prowers a transfer freight from the Fort Rouge yards to the Transcona yards in Winnipeg on March 4, 1951.

Stan F. Styles

AN EXTRA TRAIN pounds upgrade on the station bypass at Winnipeg with a mixed consist of freight but primarily pulpwood logs.

Stan F. Styles

CONSOLIDATION NO. 2505 (2-8-0) blasts upgrade toward Vancouver after having crossed the British Columbia Electric Railway Arderley crossing. The smash board is on the southbound track approaching the BCER crossing.

Stan F. Styles

CANADIAN PACIFIC WAS not alone in the practice of powering trains with Pacific type steam power. Here CN 5099 gives off a beautiful plume of smoke as she powers an eastbound extra near the Winnipeg depot.

Stan F. Styles

AN EASTBOUND FREIGHT powered by Mikado type No. 3289 pounds upgrade near the Winnipeg depot en route to Rainy River and Fort Frances, Ontario. Part of the consist of the freight is bound for the DW&P.

Stan F. Styles

A WESTBOUND WAY FREIGHT peddles across the CP-CN diamond at Matsqui, British Columbia.

Stan F. Styles

A FREIGHT TRAIN heads east out of Moncton, New Brunswick behind three models of Montreal Locomotive Works power and one Canadian Locomotive-Fairbanks Morse H-12-46, an A1A-A1A machine built only for CN and rated at 1200 horsepower. This particular train carried a caboose at both the head-end as well as the rear-end.

Jim Scribbins

A HIGH SPEED freight rolls through Portage la Prairie, Manitoba behind a trio of SD-40's with 63 cars, most of which are piggybacks and auto-racks.

Jim Scribbins

EXTRA 5136 EAST DRUNS across a curved steel deck viaduct 2 miles south of Lytton, British Columbia. Photographed by Elmer Treloar on June 10, 1970.

MONTREAL FA UNITS 9456 and 9454 lead 2nd No. 440 at St. Lambert, Quebec on September 29, 1956.

George-Paterson Collection

TWO GEEPS POWER an eastbound freight in the Thompson River Canyon north of Lytton, British Columbia on August 21, 1956. Note the snow sheds that protect the railway during the winter from snow slides.

Elmer Treloar

FOUR GRAND TRUNK Western GP-9's depart Sarnia with CN freight bound for the GTW at Port Huron. Diesel power replaced the former electric engines on what is known as the "Puller" assignment. The four geeps with both CN and GTW crews make countless trips back and forth through the tunnel with freight bound for the respective countries and are still called tunnel "motors," despite the end of tunnel electrification.

Elmer Treloar

CN OWNS AND operates a fleet of lightweight geeps with flexi-coil trucks for light rail trackage. Note the small fuel tank. The 4149 is a GP-9 with a CN road class of GR-17.

Canadian National

CN 4012 IS A GP-40, a far cry from the GP-9 in the previous photo. Note the huge fuel tanks and the change from the long end as being the front end to the short end. Color schemes too changed between the construction times of GP-9's and GP-40's.

Canadian National

GP-40's themselves have changed as time rolls on. Such locomotives are now built with crew comfort cabs and modified color scheme with new safety stripes. The 9442 is shown here shortly after construction.

Canadian National

GENERAL MOTOR's LOCOMOTIVES do not have the corner on the market for the new crew comfort cabs. This MLW Industries M420 delivered to CN in May, 1973 also sports such a cab.

Canadian National

IN THIS WRITER's opinion, the new crew comfort cabs on CN are the finest locomotive cabs ever developed. Note the speedometer over the center of the cab.

Canadian National

CN now operates a vast fleet of SD-40's with the six wheel trucks. All 6 wheel truck locomotives are called "Designated Units." Such motive power are subject to additional speed restrictions, and it is not uncommon for speed limit boards to show four speed limits: railiners, passenger trains, freight trains and designated units.

Canadian National

90

THE FORTY FOOT box car was the workhorse of the CN freight car fleet for decades. This car with the Maple Leaf insignia was photographed at the West Virginia yard in April, 1974.

Patrick C. Dorin

A BOOK COULD BE written on box cars alone with all of the variations in both interior and external equipment, such as damage free compartments, cushion underframes and so on. This photo of CN 557504 is a 50 foot car equipped with a plug door and regular door for lumber service. This car shows the standard markings or lettering for CN box cars as of the present time (early 1975).

Canadian National

CN 220002 IS AN unusual mechanical refer (rebuilt from an ice refer) in that it is equipped for icing with overhead ice compartments. Note the four overhead hatches.

Canadian National

CN 235203 IS MORE typical of the mechanical refers found in Canada.

Canadian National

FLAT CARS SERVE a variety of uses including that of hauling logs for the logging industry.

Canadian National

40 FOOT FLATS CAN also be used for hauling containers.

Canadian National

CN EMPLOYS BOTH bi- and tri-level auto-rack cars for new automobiles and truck traffic. Cars are black with white lettering.

Canadian National

85 FOOT CONTAINER CAR 635377 was built in February, 1972. Note the high speed roller bearing trucks.

Canadian National

CN 880756 IS A high cube, gondola woodchip car with an 80 ton capacity, and one top hinged end door. This car is from series 880000.

Canadian National

65 FOOT LOW SIDE mill type gondola CN 155049 as built and lettered in May, 1958.

Canadian National

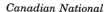

CN 137094 IS A 50 foot low side gondola.

Canadian National

LOGS OR PULPWOOD for the paper mills make up a substantial amount of CN traffic in Ontario and Minnesota. CN has equipped a number of gondolas with steel stakes for pulpwood loading in the North Country. This equipment was photographed on the DW&P at West Virginia yard.

Patrick C. Dorin

92

40 FOOT, 82 TON capacity coal gondolas are operated in coal service in Eastern Canada.

Patrick C. Dorin

CN 70 TON TRIPLE coal hopper, built in March, 1944 is painted with the large CN that no one can miss. Photographed at West Virginia, Minnesota in April, 1974.

Patrick C. Dorin

82½ TON CAPACITY coal hopper built in August, 1964.

Patrick C. Dorin

70 TON COAL hopper in the original box car red and white lettering color scheme.

Patrick C. Dorin

84 TON OPEN hopper rebuilt by CN in November, 1971.

Patrick C. Dorin

A NUMBER OF CN open hoppers have been equipped with modified or portable covers for traffic that must not be exposed to the weather. This particular car has not yet received its number.

Canadian National

93

CN 100 TON CYLINDRICAL covered hoppers are used in a variety of services, but generally for grain and potash traffic.
Canadian National

AIR DUMP CARS are normally used in work train service, but every so often perform revenue service for gravel traffic.
Canadian National

FORTY FOOT STOCK car constructed in 1929.
Canadian National

AMONG MODEL RAILROADERS, CN's wood cabooses have been regarded as highly artistic models. They were relatively large cabooses and were assigned to individual crews, which kept them in immaculate shape.
Canadian National

ONE OF THE first steel cabooses on CN was built in a design similar to the wood cabooses already in use for decades.
Canadian National

CN's MOST MODERN cabooses ride like Pullmans with those cushion underframes, and are equipped with safety lights not only for the crews stepping off moving trains (or boarding) but also track inspection lights.
Canadian National

CN TOWBOAT Margaret Yorke was used to tow the carfloat Lansdowne between Detroit and Windsor, Ontario. The carfloat carried freight cars between the CN and GTW connections for freight service to and from the Motor City.

Elmer Treloar

CN's 95 YEAR OLD carferry Huron in the Detroit River en route from Windsor to Detroit with several carloads of pipe for the GTW connection.

Elmer Treloar

BEFORE ITS CONVERSION to a carfloat, the carferry Lansdowne arrives in Windsor, Ontario in February, 1957 through the ice with freight from the GTW in Detroit. The Lansdowne was built in 1885, and she finished her career in March, 1975, 90 years of service.

Elmer Treloar

PIGGYBACK HAS BECOME an increasing important item for Canadian National, and in many terminals loading and unloading has become an around the clock operation. CN handles a variety of different types of traffic TOFC.

Canadian National

LARGE HOIST TRUCKS load and unload containers at various terminals throughout the system.

Canadian National

CN HANDLES SOLID trains of containers to and from transoceanic ships.

Canadian National

A COMBINATION PIGGYBACK and container train zips along between Hinton and Jasper on the Edson Subidivision of the Alberta Area in CTC territory. Such trains are also known as Express trains, which are numbered in the 200 series. In addition to piggyback and container freight traffic, these trains handle CN express traffic.

Canadian National

THE MARKERS ON the caboose signify the end of the train, and according to the rules, a train is not a train without those markers displaying red to the rear.

Canadian National

CHAPTER 6

The Iron Ore Lines

The vast Canadian National Railways serves three heavy duty iron ore traffic centers. The first, and possibly the most important, is the Lake Superior District Steep Rock and Bruce Lake areas. The second is in the Lake Huron District at Depot Harbour, Ontario and the third is the relatively new Sherman Mine located on the Ontario Northland Railway. These three areas produce the bulk of the 8 to 10 million tons of iron ore traffic that the Canadian National handles annually. This traffic has generated a number of interesting operations.

Iron ore was never a big item in Canadian industry until World War II. The Steep Rock Range was not discovered until 1938, and research and prospecting was not completed until July, 1943. Upon notification by the mining companies involved that the above work was completed, the Canadian National went to work on the investigations and required surveys for the construction of the ore dock and yard facilities.

The site for the transloading of iron ore from train to boat was selected at Port Arthur, which is now Thunder Bay. The ore dock was planned to meet the following conditions:

1. To handle an annual volume of 2 million tons with a provision for future expansion.
2. To provide a minimum storage of 30,000 tons of ore.
3. To permit mixing of the ore according to the silica manganese, phosphorous and iron content and as instructed by the mining company.
4. To permit rapid loading of the ore into the boats.

Studies showed that in order to accomplish those objectives the best type of dock would be the high-level, pocket type ore dock such as was operated by the Duluth, Missabe & Iron Range Railway, the Lake Superior & Ishpeming Railroad and others. At the time of construction, the ore dock was 600

feet long with 50 pockets on each side. The pockets are on 12 foot centers and can hold approximately 300 tons of ore. Canadian National ore cars are built in the same manner as ore cars on the United States iron ranges and are 24 feet long. This means that the cars unload into every other pocket. The width of the ore dock is 64 feet, 8 inches and the height is 82 feet, 6 inches. There are four tracks on top, two on each side serving each row of pockets. The first boat loaded at the dock in July, 1945 even though the outer end of the ore dock was not yet completed.

In 1945, the CN's ore operation was still relatively simple. The ore was crushed, screened and graded into but three classifications and loaded into 62 ton capacity ore cars. The ore was moved in either regular freight trains or ore extras from Atikokan (Steep Rock) to Neebing Yard just west of Fort William (now Thunder Bay). From this yard the cars were, and are, moved to the ore dock storage yard. At that point, ore dock switch crews would spot the cars on the dock for unloading and move empties to the ore dock yard. From there, they were returned to Neebing Yard. From Neebing they travel on to Atikokan where the cycle is repeated.

From 1945 through 1955 the iron ore business grew. 1945 shipments amounted to only 504,772 tons, but the 1955 figure was 2,265,555 tons. Facilities had to be expanded, not only at the Port Arthur dock and yards, but all the way to Atikokan.

To handle the increase in traffic, the Canadian National ordered 200 new ore cars, laid new rail in the single track main line, extended sidings and installed centralized traffic control. At the same time, the ore dock was extended another 600 feet. Most of this improvement program took place during the years 1954 and 1955.

The line west from Thunder Bay is extremely busy with up to 20 or more trains daily on the

THE HOLLOW SOUND of empty ore cars rattles across the bridge after dumping iron ore at Depot Harbour as the ore extra, powered by two SD-40's, begins the trip back to Moose Mountain for more iron ore. The photo was taken near Depot Harbour, Ontario on May 25, 1973.

Elmer Treloar

single track line. As one travels west ward from Thunder Bay, the first 30 miles are through farming country. Beyond that point the terrain becomes so rough and rocky that there is no agriculture or industry except for some mining activities and pulp wood cutting for paper mills. Basically there is one time freight in each direction daily between Atikokan and Thunder Bay, which is known as the Kashabowie Subdivision of the Lakehead Area. During the 1950's there was a daily passenger train in each direction but in 1974 there is only a tri-weekly RDC service between Thunder Bay and Winnipeg. Way freights are operated twice weekly in each direction. Extra trains are operated as required for grain and ore which brings the amount of traffic up to the 20 or more per day. All trains are operated as extras except for the passenger trains and a small number of trains to and from the Graham Subdivision which leaves the main line at Conmee.

At Thunder Bay, Lake Superior is 603 feet above sea level, while the tracks are about 608 feet elevation. From Thunder Bay to Shabaqua the CN follows the valley of the Kaministiquia River with a maximum grade of 1.08 per cent. From Shabaqua the ascending grade is about 1.18 per cent for four miles to mile post 57.1. At that point the grade continues to ascend at a maximum of 0.96 per cent

for 2 more miles to Annex with the next 37 miles being nearly level to Huronian. From Huronian to Atikokan the grade descends with about half of the severity of the west ward grade to Annex. Nevertheless this grade east ward from Atikokan presented a number of operating problems during the days of steam. For the east bound movement of grain and ore, the ruling grade is 0.70 per cent for the 45 miles from Atikokan to Huronian, and then level to Annex and down grade for the last 60 miles into Thunder Bay.

Much of this section of railroad is on curves. There are over 300 curves many of which range over 5 or 6 degrees and some are 8 degrees and there is one curve at 9 degrees. The maximum authorized speed is 50 miles per hour for passenger trains (which is faster than the speed authorized in 1955) and 35 miles per hour for freight trains except for the 27 miles between Conmee and Neebing Yard where the limit is 45 miles per hour. Speed is restricted substantially on the curves with some areas posting only a 20 miles per hour limit. Ore trains and trains handling ore are limited to a top speed of 30 miles per hour all the way from Atikokan to Thunder Bay.

As we stated previously, ore is usually moved in solid trains or with cars of grain. Previous to diesel locomotive operations, an east bound crew

98

A LOADED IRON ORE train rumbles over the bridge near Depot Harbour after completing a round trip to Moose Mountain for ore. All CN ore cars in the Depot Harbour, Ontario service are equipped with high sides.

Elmer Treloar

would take enough tonnage to fill out the locomotive tonnage rating from Atikokan up the hill 45 miles to Huronian where the entire set of cars was set out. The crew would then return to Atikokan and pick up the rest of the train and return to Huronian. The two sets of cars would be coupled together and the train would continue on to Port Arthur. The total tonnage would amount to about 9,500 tons which the steam locomotive could easily handle on the descending grades. With diesel locomotives, this particular operation has been discontinued.

Because of the speed restrictions due to the curves and grades and the 30 miles per hour for loaded ore cars, the overall average speed on the subdivision was low. When traffic is at the normal summer volume as many as 19 meets can be made during an 8 hour shift. Prior to 1955 when the CN operated the line by time table and train order and with hand thrown switches, much time was lost in getting in and out of sidings and waiting for meets. With a new Centralized Traffic Control System for the territory from Conmee to Atikokan, meets are often so close that neither train stops. The average speed of the subdivision was raised somewhat and is close to that governed by the curves and grades. The double track section from Conmee to Thunder

Bay has been equipped with an automatic block signal section with right hand running.

The Canadian National's Atikokan ore run serves two mining companies, the Steep Rock Iron Mines and the Caland operation. Caland is a more recent development which began operation of a million ton pellet plant in 1965-1966. To accommodate the pellet traffic, the CNR rebuilt an entire fleet of ore cars with high sides, similar to the rebuilding program that the Burlington Northern is now employing with their ore car fleet. Most of the traffic from Atikokan moves through the original pocket ore dock built at Port Arthur. It is largely a seasonal operation with traffic coming to a halt when Lake Superior freezes over. This is not the case, however, with the Canadian National's other Lake Superior District iron ore operation.

THE BRUCE LAKE, ONTARIO OPERATION

In 1968 a new pelletizing plant and iron ore mine went into operation at Bruce Lake, Ontario. This area is north west of Thunder Bay and the mine is located 253 miles from Lake Superior via Canadian National trackage. The new mine is served by a 67 mile branch off the main line at

ALL ORE EN ROUTE to the docks at Thunder Bay arrives at Neebing Yard for weighing and classification. It is then moved by transfer crews to the Hillyard or Mission yard for unloading at the ore docks. This photo shows steam switcher 8433 pulling a transfer of iron ore from Neebing yard to Hillyard in Port Arthur. The train has been weighed and classified, and the cars will shortly be dumped on the ore dock. The photo was taken on May 21, 1959 by A. Robert Johnson.

SINCE DIESELIZATION ORE transfers are powered by two or three unit combinations between Neebing and either the Hillyard or Mission yard. The latter is a new facility serving the Valley Camp dock in former Fort William. This train has just completed weighing and is en route to the Mission yard in July, 1974.

Patrick C. Dorin

THE HILLYARD AT Thunder Bay consists of 8 tracks. Of all the ore dock yards in the Lake Superior Region it is the smallest. Transfers arrives here from the Neebing yard, and both ore and coal is stored here until called for dumping by the ore dock agent. On the day this photo was taken in June, 1974, there were eight cars of coal and 36 cars of ore awaiting dumping.

carry up to 100 tons of pelletized iron ore. The top hatch is mechanically opened and closed by rubber tire devices, which are activated by two guiding runners at the loading site. There are three trains of 35 cars each. The extra 15 cars are used to replace cars taken out of service under a planned maintenance program.

These ore cars have another unusual feature and that is load-adjusting brakes. When a full load is aboard, an auxiliary set of brakes come into play so that stopping distance for a full train remains nearly the same as for that of an empty train.

The Sherman produces approximately 1 million tons annually and all of it moves via the Ontario Northland-Canadian National Railway. The maximum speed for loaded trains is 30 miles per hour over both railroads while 40 mph is permitted for empty movements. The three trains move in a 72 hour cycle with one train loading at the mine every 24 hours. A good deal of the time the cars are at the steel mill being unloaded, inspected and cars changed out for the maintenance program. The operation is a very profitable one for the Canadian National and the Ontario Northland Railways.

There are other ore movements on the Canadian National. For example in 1955 a new iron ore mine and beneficiating plant at Marmora, Ontario began operation. The mine and plant is operated by the Marmoraton Mining Company, a subsidiary of Bethlehem Steel Company. The plant produces approximately 500,000 tons annually which is shipped over the CN to Picton, Ontario 64 miles away for lake shipment. The ore dock is located on Lake Ontario and is a belt conveyor loading system. The dock is 765 feet long with a 63,000 ton storage capacity. It was built in 1955. The Canadian National has assigned a fleet of about 75 ore cars and two diesel locomotives to this ore train operation.

Altogether the CN ships ore over a total of four docks, three of which are conveyor belt facilities and only one a pocket type dock. The latter was the last dock of its type built on the Great Lakes. The pocket dock is the fastest loading ore dock, but is limited for train operations during the shipping season only. The other docks can accept pellets for storage during the entire winter season. The Sherman mine is also a year around operation. The Canadian National Railway is the only line that presently serves three ports for the transloading of iron ore from train to boat. This is a distinction that was once held only by the Soo Line Railroad.

102

TRANSFER CREWS ALSO spot the ore cars on the ore docks for unloading. This photo shows two GP-9's spoting ore for the last boat of the shipping season at the Port Arthur ore dock.
Canadian National

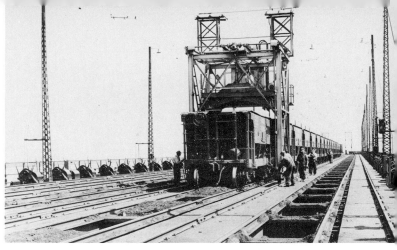

THE CN DOCK was the last pocket ore dock constructed on the Great Lakes. The Port Arthur facility is equipped with electric car shakers of the gantry type. The 24 foot ore cars line up perfectly over every other pocket, which are on 12 foot centers.
Elmer Treloar

The Canadian National's ore operations add a tidy sum of money to the cash register every year. Not only are the ore trains interesting from an operating department view point, but they keep the accounting department happy too. The ore operations are not of the magnitude of the Duluth, Missabe & Iron Range Railway in Northern Minnesota, but Canada has become a world leader in iron ore production and who knows what the future holds for Canadian National. And all of this has happened since 1944 when the Steep Rock Iron Mines began shipping over the Canadian National Railways.

ONCE THE ORE or coal is dumped into the pockets, it sometimes must be prodded in order to flow smoothly from the pocket into the lake carrier. These ore punchers are in the process of loading a boat. The machinery at the edge of the dock lowers the chutes into the holds of the freighters or ore boats as they are commonly called.
Patrick C. Dorin

THE VALLEY CAMP facility is a conveyor belt operation with the pellets stock piled prior to loading into boats. The Valley Camp dock is located in old Fort William and is served by the Mission yard. Canadian Pacific and Canadian National are presently engaged in a joint operation for a new coal dock operation for the movement of western coal to eastern markets. The new facility is not yet in operation, but will handle about 5 million tons of coal annually.
Canadian National

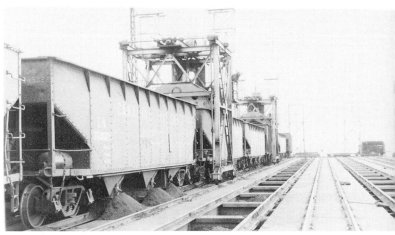

COAL IS FREQUENTLY dumped in the ore dock at Thunder Bay. This photo shows the car shakers working on 70 ton coal hoppers on top of the dock on a foggy day in June, 1974.
Patrick C. Dorin

ORE FROM THE mines is handled in solid trains of ore cars. Such trains operate in both directions, such as ore Extra 4499 West shown here preparing to depart Neebing yard with 78 empty ore cars for the Caland pellet plant at Atikokan. The photo was taken in July, 1974.

Patrick C. Dorin

PRIOR TO EXTRA 4499 West's departure from Neebing, three units came charging into the yard with 65 empty ore cars from the Hillyard in former Port Arthur.

Patrick C. Dorin

EXTRA 4499 WEST departed Neebing at 3:35 PM and was soon rolling west along the fine double track of the Kashabowie Subdivision between Neebing and Conmee. Note the welded rail and excellent track structure. Looking back along the train there is not a ripple in the consist the track is so smooth.

Patrick C. Dorin

AT 5:25 PM THE ORE extra came to a halt on the main line for a meet with train No. 308, running as Extra 5588 East. At exactly 5:26 PM 308 sailed into the siding at Rossmere.

Patrick C. Dorin

NO. 308 WAS IN the clear about 2 minutes later with two modern cabooses (both styles) as the rear end crew gave cheerful waves on the beautiful July, 1974 afternoon.

Patrick C. Dorin

A FEW MINUTES later at 6:10 PM, Extra 4499 West crept up the siding at Postans (just 11 miles from Rossmere) to await a meet with an eastbound ore extra, shown here racing by on the main line with 86 cars of ore from Atikokan.

Patrick C. Dorin

A FEW MOMENTS LATER the caboose cleared the switch and the dispatcher threw the switch and the drawf signal turned green clearing the way for the westbound ore extra to continue on its way.

Patrick C. Dorin

EXTRA 4499 WEST WOULD have one more meet at 7:05 PM with an eastbound grain Extra 5223 East at Quetico about 35 miles from Atikokan.

Patrick C. Dorin

THE SCENERY ALONG the Kashabowie Subdivision is simply spectacular with horseshoe curves and miles and miles of forest lands, lakes, streams and swamp lands. This photo shows the tale end of Extra 4499 West just a few miles from the train's destination at Atikokan. At that point, the empty ore cars were immediately taken to Caland to be loaded with ore (pellets). The cars returned to Atikokan about 1 AM, at which time a crew was called for an ore extra east to Neebing Yard. The 78 cars spent exactly 4 hours, 30 minutes between arrival and departure at Atikokan. CN's ore car utilization is exceptionally high as this same group of ore cars will be rolling west again tomorrow afternoon.

Patrick C. Dorin

THE FIRST ORE cars constructed for Canadian National came from National Steel Car Corporation at Hamilton, Ontario in 1944. These 62½ ton capacity cars were only slightly smaller than the larger ore cars constructed after the war. This ore car equipment can be operated on any railroad ore dock in the Lake Superior Region including the Chicago & North Western Railway's new dock at Escanaba, Michigan.

National Steel Car Corp.

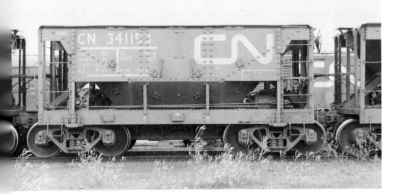

THE ORIGINAL FLEET of 62½ ton cars have all been modified somewhat for a slightly larger capacity of 68 tons. Many of the cars have been rebuilt with 18 inch extensions, and all of course now carry the new lettering arrangement. This photo was taken in Thunder Bay in July, 1974.

Patrick C. Dorin

TWO MONTREAL LOCOMOTIVE Works 2400 horsepower roadswitchers power the first unit train of pellets to the Dofasco Plant at Hamilton, Ontario. Note the pine tree atop of the first car, which is a traditional ceremony for the first carload of ore to leave a mine.

Canadian National

THE 82½ TON CAPACITY ore cars have been rebuilt with 18 inch extensions for a greater capacity. This photo shows CN ore cars being loaded with pellets.

Canadian National

CN AND ONR ORE cars are of the covered hopper variety, and are the most unusual of all equipment operated in ore service. The two wheels atop of the car serve in the automatic opening and closing of the car in a non-stop loading operation. These ore cars are the biggest operated anywhere in the Lake Superior-Huron iron ore districts.

Canadian National

NOT ALL IRON ore traffic is handled in specialized ore cars or in all ore or unit trains. This extra west to Toronto has 21 cars of iron ore pellets from the Marmora, Ontario mine. The remainder of the train is made up of general freight. Extra 6163 West was photographed near Oshawa, Ontario on March 23, 1959. Generally the ore would have gone to Picton for lake shipment, but the shipping season had not yet opened and this shipment is all rail for Buffalo, New York.

George-Paterson Collection

FINALLY NOT ALL ore traffic on CN is iron ore traffic. In the Sudbury, Ontario area, copper and nickel ores are transported in combination drop bottom-side dump ore cars with an inside length of 22 feet.

Dale Wilson

CHAPTER 7

Grain Traffic

One of the biggest work loads for Canadian National is the grain movement. Historically this has been true since before the days of the Canadian National consolidations. In fact, somewhere in the vicinity of 25% of the total annual tonnage hanled by Canadian National is grain, and this does not include such products as flour, soy beans and other grain products. This grain tonnage accounts for only about 10% of the gross revenue. (Soybeans are not a grain as such, but the transportation of them is basically the same.)

The operating procedures for the transportation of grain has not changed much during the past few decades, except for the change from steam to diesel power.

Historically, most of the grain in Canada has moved in a combination rail-water transportation arrangement. About two thirds or more of the grain moves through the port of Thunder Bay, while the rest moves to inland points or Vancouver with a very small percentage going to Churchill on Hudson Bay. A small amount of grain travels by rail east of Lake Superior, although this amount has increased in recent years particularly during the winter time.

Rail operating procedures have followed a cycle something like this. Empties are gathered together in trains for movement from Thunder Bay to Winnipeg. At Winnipeg the trains are broken down, if necessary, and are dispatched for the further distribution of empties to various points which include Regina, Brandon, Melville, Biggar, Humboldt, Dauphin, Saskatoon and many other points in Alberta, Manitoba and Saskatchewan.

Empties from the west coast are also distributed to the same points. Upon arrival, the empties are switched into other trains that take them to the local elevators all along the various lines throughout the grain producing region. Once loading of the cars is completed, trains pick up the loads and return them to the above mentioned points. They are then assembled into grain trains and dispatched to Thunder Bay, Vancouver and Churchill. Churchill handles less than 3% of the total grain shipped during their 13 week shipping season.

On the surface of it all, it would appear that the grain transportation is relatively simple. However it is more than just the distribution of empties and the picking up of loads. As of the present time, and this has been so for nearly all of the history of grain handling, there is a substantial amount of switching. At each town there may be more than one grain elevator, which may belong to more than one company. However for the purpose of getting the trains over the road, the loads are picked up as they are on the sidings. By the time a train moves over a subdivision, the various loads are all mixed up throughout the train. This entails classification work at Thunder Bay, Winnipeg, Edmonton or Vancouver. This is not only time consuming, but curtails the efficient use of freight equipment which is always in short supply. Canadian National is, however, using a pooling system that eliminates some of this extra handling of freight equipment.

Prior to the pick up of a loaded car of grain, the elevator classifies or grades the grain. A request is then made to the railway to pick up the car, and with the prior classification or grading, the cars can be switched together in a train without regard to initial shipper or the receiver. In other words, the Canadian Wheat Board tells the railway that it will ship a certain number of cars of a certain type of grain for a particular destination. The grain movement is coordinated by the Canadian Wheat Board and the Canadian Transport Commission, and tonnage or traffic targets or goals are set for both railways for the movement of designated amount of traffic during a certain time period.

Rolling stock has always been a problem, not only for Canadian National but all grain handling railroads. For one thing there is the matter of clean cars. Grain doors have been a headache for dec-

GRAIN ELEVATORS ALL over western Canada load thousands upon thousands of bushels into box cars and covered hoppers for movement to Thunder Bay or the west coast.

Canadian National

ades, but until the covered hopper car was recognized as a suitable grain carrying car, the disposable grain door was the only economical method for handling the problem. These grain doors were placed inside the steel door of the box car with an opening at the top. It created a big bin out of the car and grain was loaded with spouts at the elevator.

Paper is used for 75% of the grain doors, which are usually destroyed during unloading. Most of the remainder grain doors are constructed of wood with an average of 3½ trips. Unloading at the old shovel house terminals means that the machinery is chopping through the grain door to unload the car.

As stated before, over two thirds of all grain handled moves through Thunder Bay. In 1974 that meant 99,443 carloads. During that same year, 55,020 carloads went through the west coast, prinicipally to Vancouver, while 10,491 went to Churchhill.

Box cars are still the main type of equipment operated for grain traffic. However, the covered hopper car is becoming more and more noticable in the consist of grain trains. Never has there been a more suitable car for this type of traffic.

108

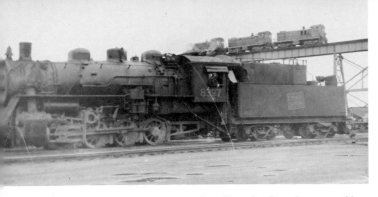

CN MAINTAINS A grain yard at Thunder Bay (between old Fort William and Port Arthur) for the movement of grain to the elevators. This photo was taken during the days of steam on an exceptional cloudy and dreary day at the Canadian Lakehead. The 0-8-0 No. 8397 stands ready to resume the switching of grain at the Port Arthur yard, while in the background 3 diesel switchers drift back to the Hillyard after shoving 50 carloads of iron ore on the ore dock.

A. Robert Johnson

MOST GRAIN TRAINS originate or terminate in the Neebing Yard west of Thunder Bay. Transfer crews then handle the grain to either the former Fort William or the Port Arthur grain elevators. This transfer is approaching the Port Arthur yard with 80 cars of grain. The ore dock can be seen in the background.

Patrick C. Dorin

GRAIN IS HANDLED in solid train loads from the western wheat fields to Thunder Bay. Such a train is Extra 5034 East standing ready to move after changing crews at Atikokan, Ontario. The consist includes 123 box cars of grain destined for the elevators at Thunder Bay. She departed Atikokan at 3:35 AM and arrived at Neebing Yard at 8:00 AM. The grain extra met four trains including symbol freight No. 307, one ore extra and two empty grain trains between Atikokan and Neebing. This July, 1974 night is cool and crisp with a light fog.

Patrick C. Dorin

THE CANADIAN GOVERNMENT leases a fleet of 100 ton capacity grain hoppers to both Canadian National and Canadian Pacific. This equipment has eased the car shortages somewhat.

Canadian National

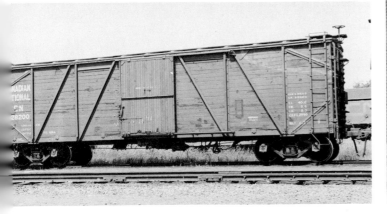

WOOD BOX CARS can still be seen in the consist of grain trains in 1975.

Patrick C. Dorin

WHEN BOX CARS and grain hoppers are in short supply, standard open hoppers are cleaned and fitted with covers for the movement of grain.

Canadian National

CHAPTER 8

The Electric Interurban Lines

A railway as large as Canadian National is bound to contain the widest variety of equipment, services and styles of operation to be found anywhere. Observing the Turbo gliding down the rails at 95 miles per hour, or an express train kicking up the dust at 65 per or heavy grain, coal and ore trains would give little hint that the CNR was once an electric interurban railway operator.

Five of the more important services included the Montreal and Southern Counties Railway; the Niagara St. Catharines & Toronto Railway District; the Toronto Suburban District, the Quebec Railway and the Oshawa Street Railway. The last of these lines to join Canadian National was the Quebec Railway, purchased in 1951 for $750,000.

None of these lines took on the magnitude of the North Shore or South Shore in the Chicago area or the Pacific Electric in Los Angeles, each of which once operated over 90 miles of line. However, these lines offered the traveling public a frequent, fast service over their routes.

The most extensive of the interurban services was the Montreal and Southern Counties Railway. Furthermore, it was once the key transportation network in Canada's largest city. The railway was originally chartered on June 29, 1897, and it was amended in 1898, 1902, 1905 and 1910. Few companies can brag about it taking 13 years for something to be done with the charter after it was obtained. However, before we get too far ahead of ourselves, we should take a brief look at the first transportation system between Montreal and the South Shore area.

In 1904 a bus service, the very first in Canada, was inaugurated by the Montreal & South Shore Auto Car Co. The company operated five buses, two of which were closed and three were open. The bus route started at Victoria Square and followed St. James St. and finally crossed the Victoria Bridge. The line terminated on Aberdeen Ave in St. Lambert. However, the bus line soon gave up as

the streets and roads in Montreal and St. Lambert were so bad that operation was totally impractical.

The Montreal & Southern Counties Railway then had their charter amended to take over the bus company and replace it with an electric railway. It is probably one of just a few instances where bus transportation succumbed to a railway.

In order to build a railway between Montreal and the South Shore of the St. Lawrence River, it was necessary to have a bridge or ferry crossing. The most practical solution was to secure permission to use the Victoria Bridge of the Grand Trunk Railway. The Grand Trunk agreed, and after extensive opposition by the Montreal Street Railway, construction began. At the same time Grand Trunk secured the controlling interest of stock in the new line and in turn financed the construction of the railroad.

Construction began in 1909 and service was started on Nov. 1, 1909 between Montreal and St. Lambert with 2 passenger cars. The complete line to Granby (47.45 miles from Montreal) was completed on April 30, 1916. The last new construction was the electrification of a short piece of track to St. Angele in 1926, and this was the last new electrification of a railway in Canada up to the present time.

One of the interesting points about the M&SC is that there was a joint operation of steam and electric trains over a portion of the route. (Note model railroaders, we now have a prototype to operate interurban cars on the same track with main line trains.) Because of this it was necessary for the M&SC to be operated by standard rules in use on steam railroads, and the practice continued for many years after 1925 when the steam operation was re-routed.

The company operated with direct current electric power for all of its history. At first, it was purchased from the Grand Trunk's Point St. Charles Shops, generated by steam, from 1909 to

1913. From that date to the end of operations power was purchased from the Quebec Hydro Electric Company.

For most of the company's career an excellent suburban passenger service was provided with trains running between St. Lambert, Montreal South, Greenfield Park, Mackayville and Montreal every twenty minutes. Four trains daily in each direction were operated between Montreal and Granby with additional service between Brookline, Marieville and Montreal. A way freight operated each way daily furnishing service between Granby and Montreal.

Express service also operated three times each way daily between Montreal and Brandy as well as twice daily mail service with letter boxes on the cars.

As of the early 1950's, the M&SC operated the following roster:

Passenger Cars	47
Baggage & Express	5
Locomotives	2
Work and Miscellaneous Cars	14

Despite the good service, the road never really obtained a profitable operation. In only one year from 1916 to 1955 did the road covers its bond interest. The road did earn a slight profit of about a 5% return on the investment during the late 1920's, but from 1931 on the railway incurred operating losses annually. The operating ratio was 142% in 1949 and it reached 200% in 1953. The road had passed into the Canadian National family with the Grand Trunk, but it never achieved much status of any kind. In many ways it was a forgotten orphan. The electric service from Merieville to Granby was halted in 1951, and the final electric car to operate from Montreal departed McGill Street in June, 1955. For a short while, CN operated shuttle trains between Montreal and St. Lambert to connect with M&SC suburban cars still running on the south shore, but that too was discontinued in December, 1955 with a private bus operator then using the roadway which replaced the M&SC tracks on the Victoria Bridge. A great but highly unprofitable, electric railway was laid to rest, but most of the lines continue to be used for CN freight service.

The Niagara, St. Catharines & Toronto Railway District became part of Canadian National from the big road's organization. During the 1920's the District operated four routes as follows:

MONTREAL AND SOUTHERN COUNTIES electric interurban train arrives at Granby. Service to Granby began in April, 1916.

Canadian National Railways

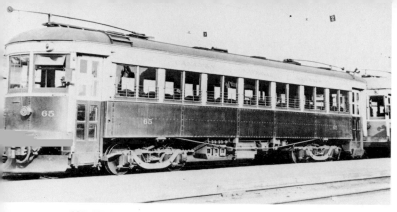

NStC&T ELECTRIC CAR, marked "Canadian National Railway," No. 65 lays over between runs at Niagara Falls, Ontario in August, 1934.

Paul Stringham

WOODEN INTERURBAN CARS were in service on many lines including CN's NStC&T. Such a car was the 131 marked "Canadian National Electric Railway," shown here at St. Catharines, Ontario on August 19, 1934.

Paul Stringham

A NStC&T LINE CAR crew repairs the overhead wire at Thorold, Ontario.

Elmer Treloar

St. Catharines, Ont. to Niagara Falls	12.8 miles
Thorold, Ont. to Port Colborne	18.8 miles
St. Catharines to Port Dalhousie	5.0 miles
St. Catharines to Niagara-on-the-Lake	12.2 miles

In 1926, service to and from Niagara Falls was hourly or even more frequent from 6:00 AM until 1:00 AM in both directions. The Port Colborne line service frequency was hourly from 6:00 AM to about 11:25 PM in both directions. The Port Dalhousie line offered the most frequent service of any of the four routes. Indeed, it was the most complicated. Service began at 5:45 AM and hourly service began at 8:00 AM. Beginning at 12:30 PM, trains ran every 30 minutes until 8:30 PM from which time trains ran every hour until 12:30 AM. Service on the Niagara-on-the-Lake line was the least frequent. It began at 6:00 AM and achieved 90 minute frequency from 9:00 AM to 12:00 Noon. From then until 5:15 trains ran every 45 minutes. From 5:15 PM until 12:15 AM there were but four trains in each direction. The rolling stock resembled the usual interurban, and the cars carried either "Canadian National Railways" or "Canadian National Electric Railways" in the letter boards. Because of the short distance involved, parlor and dining car service was never offered.

As would be expected, the Great Depression and the automobile teamed up to kill the service on the four lines. By 1953 only the Thorold-Port Colborne route still operated and with hourly service from 6 AM to 11 PM. The St. Catherines-Port Dalhousie route was replaced with bus service which operated every thirty minutes from 6 AM until 12 Midnight in both directions. The St. Catherines-Niagara Falls run was also replaced by hourly bus service from 6:05 AM until 1:00 AM in both directions. By 1959, the Thorold-Port Colborne route was expanded to a St. Catherines-Port Colborne via Thorold with a bus service seven times daily in each direction. The rail interurban service was part of history. The bus service was operated by Canadian National Transportation Limited, and therefore rail tickets were honored. However, by the year 1965 Lakeview Bus Service took over the operation, with but one bus each way daily. Rail tickets were not honored. From 1971 the service no longer appeared in CN passenger time tables. The history of the electric lines in the Niagara Peninsula, and the subsequent bus service had

A NIAGARA, St. Catherines & Toronto Ry electric car arrives at Port Colborne, Ontario on August 1, 1957.
Elmer Treloar

come to a close. With the current energy problems, this writer wonders how many people wish the service still existed.

The Toronto Suburban District was more of a main line or heavy duty type of operation. The district extended from the St. Clair Avenue & Keele Street Station in Toronto to the Guelph, Ontario Canadian National Railway station. The distance was 49.4 miles, whereas the longest line in the Niagara Peninsula was 18.8 miles. Service began at 6:30 AM from Toronto. The next train departed at 8:30 AM and finally at 10:30 AM service began on an every two hour frequency until 11:00 PM. Service from Guelph began at 6:20 AM with the next train at 9:00 AM and every two hours from then until 11:00 PM. There were 13 intermediate stops and a running time of two hours according to the May 2, 1926 time table. The principal intermediate stops were Georgetown and Acton. Again the equipment was not of the First Class variety, and offered only coach seat service along the route. Indeed, the line did not even offer a suitable commuter service as the first train did not arrive at Toronto until after 8:00 AM. After working hours departures were at 4:30 and 6:30 PM. This could hardly be considered a commuter service except for the 9 to 4 crowd, and since most people work from 8 to 4 or 5, or 9 to 5 the Toronto Suburban District was not a reliable form of transportation as such. It was, however, great for shoppers, cultural events, movies and sporting events. Indeed additional trains were run on weekends during the summer times for all kinds of activities including family picnics. Nevertheless, the Toronto Suburban District too fell victim to the Great Depression and the Automobile.

The most recent of the CN interurbans was the only railway (or one of very few) that has an ecclesiastical blessing. The Quebec Railway operated between Quebec City and St. Joachim and served the famous shrine of Ste. Anne de Beaupre. The shrine itself played a very important part in the railway's construction. Back tracking a little, the shrine was built in thanksgiving by a group of Breton sailors who were caught in a fierce thunder storm. The sailors vowed that if they came through the storm safely, they would build a church dedicated to the grandmother of Jesus of Nazereth. This church was built in 1658 and by 1844 organized pilgrimages were occurring. Consequently, the Quebec, Montmorency and Charlevoix Railway was chartered in 1881, and it was completed to Ste. Anne de Beaupre on August 10, 1889. A very large inaugural ceremony was held with Cardinal Taschereau presiding. To this writer's knowledge, no other railroad ever rated the attendance of a Cardinal let alone the Cardinal actually presiding. Because of this, and the fact that the line has carried millions of passengers to and from the shrine, the railway was known as the "Chemin de fer de la bonne Ste. Anne."

As we stated earlier in this chapter, the Quebec Railway was purchased in 1951 for $750,000. The 25 mile line was actually the result of a three way

CHAPTER 9

Narrow Gauge in Newfoundland

The Newfoundland Railway did not become part of the Canadian National Railways until Newfoundland became the tenth province of Canada on April 1, 1949. As it turned out, NR would be the last significant railway acquisition to be made by Canadian National. Furthermore, the line was constructed during the period from 1884 to 1910, all 796 miles of 3 foot, 6 inch gauge. This is a full 14½ inches smaller than standard gauge.

Upon takeover by the CNR, Newfoundland Railway operated 46 steam engines, three diesel engines, assorted freight, passenger and work equipment, and a run down track and right of way. Moreover, except for World War II, the NR barely earned its own way. Yet Canadian National looked positively on the railway with the possibility of new traffic for the main land.

Initially progress was slow. The railway had to be studied and analyzed before money could be poured into it for reconstruction. However two projects were obvious. The track had to be rebuilt, and secondly, steam power would have to be replaced by diesel power. Indeed, 53 diesel units of two classes would be purchased from 1952 through 1960 to replace the previous smaller number of steam. This purchase reflected both an improved service and increases in freight traffic. Usually, the purchase of diesel power meant fewer pieces of motive power rather than a greater number as occurred on Newfoundland.

When one looks at the Newfoundland Railway, the width of the track and equipment size does not seem out of place. Railway observers might note that the floors of the cars seem to be closer to the rail than is the case with standard gauge equipment. There are a number of standard gauge 40 foot steel box cars on 3'6" trucks permanently, and their appearance in a train is not much different from the sight of the 80 and 90 foot "hi-cube" auto parts box cars in mainland freights. Some of the converted cars on the island are captive cars. They were assigned to island service and do not cross the Cabot Strait. Originally there were no car ferries to the Island. Freight to and from Newfoundland was transferred from rail to ship to rail, a very expensive procedure. However after 1967, rail car ferries began service to Port aux Basques. Upon arrival at the port, the standard gauge trucks are exchanged for narrow gauge trucks for freight delivery throughout the island. Thus the number of car transfers has been reduced from two to none per trip.

Freight equipment is made up of log flats, wood and steel box cars, tank cars, gondola and hopper cars, stock cars, refrigerator cars and of course the reliable caboose. Equipment is not unlike the mainland.

Rail passenger service still exists on the island in 1974 as a number of mixed trains. There are four sets of mixed runs as follows: 203 and 204, Badger-Deer Lake; 211 and 212, Brigus Jct.-Carbonear; 207 and 208/232, St. Johns-Argentia; and 205 and 206 between Clarenville and Bonavista. Through passenger service between St. Johns and Port-aux-Basques is now handled by CN bus service with local and express service with the latter known as the "Expedo."

Before we get into some of the present day bus and freight operations, let's drift back to the mid-1960's when heavy passenger trains still rolled over the former Newfoundland Railway.

The passenger cars of the Newfoundland Area were about the size of heavy weight interurban cars. The vestibules were much smaller than standard gauge equipment, and the ceilings were lower. Vestibules doors were of the Dutch door variety and notices were posted warning people not to throw cigarette butts from the train due to danger of forest fires. Strangely enough there were no notices to stay out of the vestibules and not to open doors.

The sleeping cars were of the eight section, one drawing room design. Berths were shorter than those in mainland cars with limited headroom in the uppers, but oddly enough with more headroom in the lowers as compared to standard gauge cars.

As with standard "Pullman" practice, there were two windows per section. Lighting within the sections were of the bare bulb design which had disappeared prior to the construction of the last pre-Depression heavy weight sleepers on the mainland. However the aisle overhead fixtures were more modern. Berths, naturally, were narrower than those of the mainland equipment. During the mid-1960's, the sleepers were being repainted in the new image scheme. The interior colors went from a green interior to a blue-grey combination.

The dining cars included four tables seating two on the right side of the car, and four tables for four on the left. The kitchen took up half the space of the car. The interior decor resembled many heavy weight diners which had been slightly modernised.

All coaches had reclining seats, although not as wide and spaced a little closer regarding leg room than their mainland cousins. There was a slight difference in coach construction. The lowered numbered cars contained an older seat design. The higher number cars had a streamlined interior with seats (except for size) identical to the newest mainland coaches. The exterior of the latter had a very smooth streamlined appearance, while the former had a modern contour but with riveted sides and a heavier air about them than do most streamlined cars.

All passenger equipment had round ceilings with the same type of overhead aisle lighting fixtures. There were ventilators in the ceilings (through which the wind made quite a noise at times), screened windows in the end doors to admit air from the vestibules and Baker heaters. None of the cars had tight lock couplers and the slack action was appreciable on the curves and grades. None of the cars were air conditioned.

All head end cars were of the streamlined riveted design and had Baker heaters. However nearly all passenger trains carried a steam generator car of smooth streamlined exterior. So the individual car heaters were probably used for emergencies only.

The average passenger consist was once about 10 cars on the average. A typical make up in the mid-1960's might include two diesel units, steam generator car, express car, diner (as lounge car), three or four coaches, diner, sleeper (as dormitory for dining car crew), and two or three sleepers. Weekends would generate 17 and 18 car trains as well as passenger extras from time to time.

Passenger trains were scheduled for 21½ hours across the island. The primary train was the Caribou, trains 101 and 102, which operated daily during the summer and tri-weekly the remainder of the year. The Caribou was an interesting train, and provided passengers with an interesting and unusual trip. In order to find out what it was like, let's take a trip on the Caribou with Jim and Barbara Scribbins during the summer of 1966.

PORT AUX BASQUES is usually the first place that people arrive at when visiting Newfoundland. The island is full of contrasts with both rocky and forested areas. The yard here is a highly important one as it is the transfer point between bus and rail traffic and the ferry boats to and from the main land. Note the box cars on the head-end of the passenger train in the foreground.

Canadian National

THIS PHOTO SHOWS the Corner Brook yard looking Northeast. The photo gives one an idea of the contrasts with the hilly area to the right and the water bordering the yard on the left. Some of the freight cars give a hint to the economy with pulpwood flats, tank cars and gondolas with very few box cars. The tug out in the bay pulling a raft of pulpwood gives still a further hint to the economy in Newfoundland.

Canadian National

A TRIP ACROSS THE ISLAND

Traveling across the Cabot Strait by CNR boat, the first view of Newfoundland is of the blue-black quiet sea reflecting just a hint of the non-visible sun, huge dark green barren hills rising directly from the water, topped with a streak of orange from this same non-visible ball of fire with orange yellow brilliance melting into a grey overcast sky. A scene beautiful despite its desolate effect. The combination ship/rail passenger terminal at Port-aux-Basques is a modern brick structure with a restaurant and waiting room on the second floor, which is entered from the ship, and another waiting room at ground level. To one side is a paved street, while from the other extends a single track upon which waits the equipment of the only narrow gauge passenger train in North America which includes in its consist both sleeping and dining cars. The space between the track and street serves as a parking lot. Signs inside the terminal emphasize the increased traffic to the island, something the highway (unfortunately) has benefited more from than has the railway, though both waiting rooms are well occupied by people waiting for their 42 inch wide and up to 549 mile long journey.

The trip east is made on No. 102. The consist of the train from the rear includes sleeping cars: Fogo, Gander, Bishop Falls, Humber and Lewisporte (the latter operated as a dormitory for the dining car crew.), dining car, three coaches, dining car (serving as a lounge car), express car, two wood box express cars of storage mail, steam generator car and units 912 and 942. At Corner Brook two additional sleepers (Princeton and Whitbourne) and two coaches were added to the train. A major part of the patronage were students traveling to St. John's for the university fall term.

Prior to departure from Port-aux-Basques, passengers can view the engine terminal and the small yard from the right hand side of the train.

The entire terminal is surrounded by cliffs which the railway penetrates as soon as the train leaves the depot platform.

As the Caribou departs Port-aux-Basques, passengers can see several lakes, a small causeway, the sea on the North and mountains which are quite high but with stunted vegetation on the South. Growth close to the tracks is also stunted. Though there are not many forests in this section, neither are there many farms. Only a few sheep can be seen. Indeed the lack of farms is quite evident throughout the island.

As the train passes Doyles a wide valley is entered with the Anguilles on the North and the Long Range to the South and the growth is no longer stunted. Pine trees now predominate. Frequently the train negotiates reverse curves, and very often pairs of them. Train speed is by no means breath taking and it varies from 35 to 45 miles per hour. Sometimes the speed is even slower, and every once in awhile, the train hits the maximum of 50 mph. None of the passenger equipment have tight lock couplers, and the slack runs constantly in and out on the various grades and curves throughout the journey. After awhile, St. George's Bay can be seen on the west while the mountains continue on the other side. All of the towns are small. Most of which are flag stops and the train stops at nearly all of them. The homes and buildings are generally brightly painted.

There are several long bridges over rivers joining the bay and passengers have a final look at the water expanse between St. George's and Stephenville Crossing. Then, almost unexpectedly, the train plunges right through the mountains. Sometimes parallel to swift rocky rivers, some-times in canyons and at other times along lakes with rock-faced mountains on the far shore. The entry into Corner Brook is a long steep descent along what in Norway would be called a "fjord." As stated previously, No. 102 picks up additional cars here and is attacked from the head end and the rear as the sleepers and coaches are added. The engine doing the switching is the 927 and it becomes the third unit for this massive train now consisting of 17 cars plus the steam generator. It is a man-sized train to say the least.

Near South Brook one can see Newfoundland Railway 4-6-2 No. 593 displayed in good condition under a roofed area in Provincial Park to the north of the right of way.

The tableware in the dining car still carried the initials "NR."

It is also interesting to note that the Caribou carried no sleeping car conductors. At one time, the train conductor collected sleeping car tickets, but by 1966 each porter took care of those for his car.

Before Grand Lake is reached, train 102 has met three trains heading west. Train 203, which the locals refered to as the "postal" in 1966, was powered by three 900's with 37 freight cars, two express cars, one Rail Post Office car and a van. In addition to No. 203, 102 met an extra west and the westbound Caribou with just two units and ten passenger cars.

The mountains swing behind Deer Lake and flatten out by the time Grand Lake is reached near Howley. Between Kitty's Brook and Gaff Topsail barren hills, not seen since the vicinity of St. Andrews, reappear and the climb of the railway is edged with snow fences. The vast openess of the

AS ONE MIGHT guess, motive power in Newfoundland varied from the main land varieties, but with many similarities. For example, the Newfoundland Railway operated 30 Mikado type (2-8-2) locomotives, more than any other wheel arrangement. The Newfoundland lines also operated four Ten Wheelers, one Consolidation and ten Pacifics, all of which operated over the entire island. The 329 is shown here on the head-end of a log train at Bishops Falls, Newfoundland in November, 1954.
Harold K. Vollrath Collection

DIESELS WERE EVEN more individualistic. In 1956 six of the esthetically appealing General Motors model G-8 were delivered. They are the North American version of a basic export design, and rate 875 horsepower. When photographed in September, 1966 they appeared to be used primarily for branch line service.
Jim Scribbins

THIS SUNDAY AFTERNOON line up of power in front of shop building at St. John's in September, 1966 reveals the "new image" red-nose livery as well as the green and yellow which preceeded it and both types of diesel units. We see the geep-like NFD, of which the 946 was the final member of the class, and the smaller G-8's exemplified by the 805 and 802. The well-maintained locomotive shop was still identifiable as "Newfoundland Railway" at the time of the photo.

Jim Scribbins

area is strewn with huge boulders. At Gaff Topsail the surroundings are flat to the horizon with an occassional mesa protruding appearing for all the world like the United States southwest except for the lack of sand. This geographic condition prevails until darkness settles making it impossible to see any of the three American Smelting & Refining diesels that might happen to be at Millertown Junction.

The early riser sees some of the east end of the island before arrival at St. John's (where the engine terminal and shop are conveniently located adjacent to the station, and units and spare equipment are stored).

The Scribbins spent a brief time at St. John's before returning to Port-aux-Basques. On the day of their departure, the equipment for train 101 was backed into the large grey stone depot headquarters building approximately thirty minutes prior

to its noon departure, and passengers began to board the two sleeping cars without formal announcement. About ten minutes in advance of the highball, units 938 and 945 couple on. Behind them were steam generator car, diner (as lounge), four coaches, dining car, Lewisporte (as dormitory), Whitbourne and Princeton. The consist remained the same all the way to Port-aux-Basques.

Statistics seem to indicate that the Avalon Peninsula, where St. John's is located, is the most populated and most agrarian section. However, once clear of the capitol's area neither of these categories seem any more prevalent than on the western half of the line. Conception Bay is to the north and island infested. There are mountains to the south as the train climbs steeply westward toward Killigrews, and on toward Holyrood the mountains often stand alone. Rolling west from that town a long horseshoe curve takes the railway

IN SCENIC WESTERN Newfoundland, the 3 foot, 6 inch "Caribous" meet at the passing track designated as Cooke in the time table. Approaching in the "loop" track is train 101, while St. John's bound 102 is standing on the main track.

Jim Scribbins

THE PORTION OF THE island closest to St. John's is the Avalon Peninsula, which is more open, though still fairly rugged. West of Holyrood, train 101 rolls over the first subdivision of its cross island journey. Behind the pair of NFD's are a steam generator car in the original olive green livery, baggage car, a diner used as a snack car for coach passengers, four coaches, full service diner, sleeper as dormitory for the dining car crew. Behind the photographer were two sleepers in revenue service.

Jim Scribbins

up around and finally away from the bay and inland through rolling terrain punctuated with pine forests, occassional lakes and near Brigus Junction scattered mountains again have the mesa effect above the more open rocky surroundings of the line.

As 101 nears Placentia Junction, mixed train 207 waits just beyond the junction switch to the Argentia Subdivision. A few passengers transfer from 101 to the mixed which consists of three 800 series units, 10 freight cars, one short center door express car and an ancient looking combine.

The next ten miles brings about more stunted growth and the distant hills turn into barren mountains and the entire scene calls to mind the vastness of the West. Soon however, the mountains close in on the railway with stone faces and frequent rock cuts. There are many variations of this scenic theme, with a full pine mantel, plus the addition of good views of the inlets in the vicinity of Come-By-Change and Clarenville. At Port Blandford the railway forms the western boundary of Terra Nova National Park.

From here darkness settles over the westbound Caribou as the Scribbins eat their evening meal in the dining car. The setting was especially peaceful, and they later remarked that they thought how good it would be just to keep riding and riding on that friendly railway in Newfoundland.

Passenger service, such as described by the Scribbins continued until 1968. At the end of that

year, Canadian National inauguarted a trans-island bus service using "Road Cruisers." These buses provide a local service between St. John's and Port-aux-Basques plus an express run, the "Expedo." However before we get too far ahead of ourselves, let's take a look at some of the other passenger services between 1949 and 1968.

After take over, Canadian National operated the Caribou on a tri-weekly basis (except during the summer) between St. John's and Port-aux-Basques. During the other days of the week (tri-weekly), trains 15 and 16 filled in between St. John's and Corner Brook. Coaches, dining car and sleepers made up the consist of 1, 2, 15 and 16. By the late 1950's only the Caribou, trains 1 and 2, were running on the tri-weekly basis in the off season, and daily during the summers. There was also a daily except Sunday mixed train service across the entire island.

By the mid-1960's this changed still further. The mixed train, 203 and 204, though actually operating daily carried passengers only two days per week. Although called the "mail" or "postal" by the employees, 203 and 204 would have best been called "Time Freights." They handled about 40 freight cars, two express cars, Rail Post Office and a van. The van was also used to accommodate what passengers that did show up to ride them. 203 and 204 are still the daily time freights in 1974. Also during the mid-1960's, Canadian National operated another pair of time freights, 400 and 401,

121

THE SEMI-STREAMLINED dining car 172 was the head-end diner in use as a snack car for coach passengers on train 101 in the previous photo.

Jim Scribbins

THE SLEEPING CAR Fogo, for some unknown reason, possesses an observation platform but its interior was identical to all other Newfoundland sleeping cars, 8 sections and 1 drawing room.

Jim Scribbins

SLEEPING CAR HUMBER (an 8 section, 1 drawing room sleeper) poses in its new image color scheme for photographer Jim Scribbins.

COACH NO. 763 is being added to train 102 at Corner Brook during a September, 1966 trip for overflow traffic. Some of the coaches had all-welded smooth sides rather than riveted.

Jim Scribbins

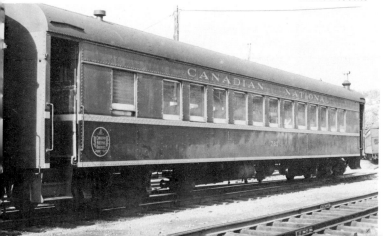

between St. John's and Port-aux-Basques. These two freights could have been considered drag freights. For example, they were scheduled for 36 hours to cross the island and one consist of No. 400 (in 1966) shows the train consist of three diesel units, 24 freight cars and 47 log flats. 400 and 401 are no longer scheduled freight trains.

Other passenger service included mixed trains 207 (Monday, Wednesday and Friday) and 208 (Tuesday, Thursday and Saturday) operated on the eastern half of the St. John's Subdivision then over the Argentia Subdivision to Argentia from Placentia Junction. The eastbound trip (208) also made a side trip over the Carbonear Subdivision from Brigus Junction to Carbonear as trains 211 and 212. The same operation still holds true today in 1975. The diversion over that branch restricts these trains to the smaller motive power of the 800 class.

Mixed trains 205 and 206 operated (and still do in 1975) over the longest branch, the Bonavista Sub extending 88 miles from its junction on the main line just west of Clarenville on a tri-weekly schedule. This line is also restricted to the 800 series units.

Passenger equipment on the various mixed trains were orange, flat roofed vehicles with open platforms. These combines have caboose size windows on their passenger ends but no cupola or bay windows.

Motive power on CNR's three foot six inch line was entirely constructed by General Motors Diesel. The 800 series are standard production model G-8's rated at 875 horsepower, and are quite in proportion to their 42 inch gauge. They are operated with their long hood forward.

The larger and older 900 series are rated 1200 hp, and are a special breed engineered by GMD for the island although they do have similarities with some of the standard export models. From the front they look like a scaled down Geep, their frame being considerably heavier than that of their standard gauge kin. It is when the cab has passed that the viewer is caught off guard for behind the "footplate" there is no short hood, only a platform resembling that of a conventional yard switcher. All motive power is clean and well maintained.

Train operation is entirely by time table and train order. There are no wayside signals, although train radio is used as an aid to movement.

The Subdivisions are as follows:

Argentia	Placentia Jct.	to Argentia
Bishop's Falls	Bishop's Falls	to Corner Brook
Bonavista	Clarenville	to Bonavista
Carbonear	Brigus Jct.	to Carbonear

ONE OF THE very few older cars seen on the island was Business Car 3, shown here adjacent to the combination ship-rail terminal at Port-aux-Basques.

Jim Scribbins

Clarenville	Clarenville	to Bishop's Falls
Lewisporte	Notre Dame Jct.	to Lewisporte
Port-aux-Basques	Corner Brook	to Port-aux-Basques
St. John's	St. John's	to Clarenville
Stephenville	Whites Road	to Stephenville

Total Newfoundland Area Mileage = 711.3 (1974)

As mentioned previously, since 1967 there has been a standard gauge operation on Newfoundland. Canadian National operates rail car ferry service to Port-aux-Basques. One switch engine is maintained at the Port to switch the car ferry. These ferries are similar to the Lake Michigan type and can carry locomotives if need be. Usually, however, there is but one standard gauge switch engine at Port-aux-Basques.

Canadian National, along with the Rio Grande, are the last two railways in North America to operate both standard and narrow gauge rail lines. Southern Pacific has long since folded up its operation and the Chicago & North Western and Milwaukee Road gave up theirs nearly a half century ago. The narrow gauge operations of the Newfoundland Area are now the largest in North America, and represent an unusual chapter in Canadian National operations and history.

THIS PHOTO SHOWS the interior of coach No. 768. As with main land coaches, those in narrow gauge operation were divided into smoking and no-smoking rooms. Reclining seats, but as with all 3 foot, 6 inch cars "air conditioning" was accomplished by opening the windows or the vents between the lighting fixtures. All passenger cars contained Baker heaters, but normally heat was furnished from the steam generator car on the head-end.

Jim Scribbins

SLEEPER BISHOP'S FALLS, 8 section, 1 drawing room car in the green, yellow and black color scheme.

Jim Scribbins

BEHIND A PAIR of NF units, train 102, the Caribou, runs parallel to the shore of one of the many lakes in western Newfoundland. This is in the subdivision between Port-aux-Basques and Corner Brook. Behind the units (lead engine in the older green livery) are steam geneator, two wooden box express cars, express car, a diner operated as a lounge car, three smooth side coaches (reclining seats), dining car, sleeper as dormitory for the dining car crew, followed by revenue sleepers from which the photo was made in September, 1966.

Jim Scribbins

EQUIPMENT FOR THE express trains seemed to be all from the 1943 re-equipping which was carried out because of the Newfoundland Railway's importance to the war effort. (The all-welded coaches obviously came in later years, most likely after NR became part of CNR when Newfoundland became a Province of Canada.) One of the few RPO's anywhere in Canada in 1966 was the 1804 pictured shortly before its departure from St. John's on the westbound express train.

Jim Scribbins

PART OF THE consist included express car 1601, coupled to RPO 1804. Note the caboose on the rear of this express train about to depart from St. John's.

Jim Scribbins

AT ONE TIME most box cars in Newfoundland were wooden, but a number of steel standard gauge cars with narrow gauge trucks were in captive service on the island. All freight from the mainland was transferred to and from ships at North Sydney and Port-aux-Basques, although track changing (mainland gauge to narrow gauge) is important today.

Jim Scribbins

MODERN STEEL VAN 6061 reflects a somewhat more advanced design than the 6058 in the previous photo. The color scheme is sort of a reddish orange with white lettering. Photographed at St. John's in September, 1966.

Jim Scribbins

CABOOSES RESEMBLE MAINLAND versions, such as the 6058 shown here at Port-aux-Basques. In the background are the rocky grey cliffs which are the visitors first sight as the ship enters the harbor.

Jim Scribbins

THE CN STEAMSHIP Bar Haven was used in Newfoundland coastal service. Much larger passenger orientated vessels cross Cabot Strait sailing between Port-aux-Basques and North Sydney, Nova Scotia. Rocky cliffs form the backdrop at Port-aux-Basques.

Jim Scribbins

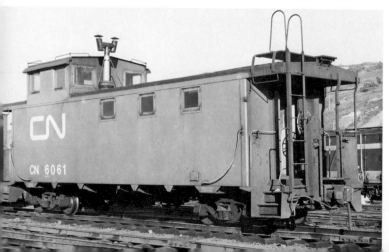

WITH THE CAR UP in the air, the standard gauge trucks are rolled away and the narrow gauge trucks are rolled in. This photo shows the workmen rolling the narrow set in under the car. The truck exchange method is substantially easier and less expensive than the old system of changing cars.

Canadian National Railways

CN NO LONGER transfers freight from standard gauge to narrow gauge equipment. In this photo CN box car has arrived in Newfoundland and is being placed into position for the exchange of the standard trucks for narrow gauge trucks. Note the jacks on both sides of the car.

Canadian National

CN PASSENGER SERVICE between St. Johns and Port-aux-Basques is now provided by buses of the type shown in this photo.

Canadian National Railways

CHAPTER 10

The Great Slave Lake Railway

One of the more unusual railway construction ventures took place not in the 1860's, but in the 1960's. This was during a time when too many people felt that the railway was on its way out as a form of transportation. Yet few people realized that Canadian National was engaged in one of the biggest railway construction projects since 1900.

CN's Great Slave Lake branch extends 377 miles from Roma Junction, on the Northern Alberta Railways, to Hay River, on the shore of Great Slave Lake, with a 54 mile branch to the huge lead-zinc ore deposits at Pine Point, North West Territories.

It was constructed originally to handle the lead and zinc concentrate from the Pine Point area, but as the construction of the line proceeded northward it was evident that a boom involving agriculture, timber and oil development was taking place. Grain elevators were constructed at Manning and sawmills and planner mills were built at various locations along the railway line. The discovery of oil in the Rainbow Lake area resulted in a tremendous surge of activity.

The Great Slave Lake line is also an important link in the transportation system servicing the Mackenzie Valley and the Arctic Coast, carrying large tonnages of northbound equipment and materials of all descriptions.

Although the line was under construction between 1961 and 1968 traffic actually began moving over it in 1964.

The entire railway is divided into three subdivisions, which are operated as part of the Alberta Area of the Mountain Region. Yet the railway is physically separated from the parent railway and connects only through the Northern Alberta Railways. This is not unlike the Great Northern Railway's California extension which connected with the parent line through the Oregon Trunk Railway. The Northern Alberta is owned on a 50/50 basis with the Canadian Pacific Railway.

The first subdivision is known as the Manning Subdivision and extends from Northern Alberta Railway Junction to High Level, 182.9 miles. Next comes the Meander River Sub from High Level to Hay River, 194.1 miles. The Pine Point Sub leaves the Meander Sub at Pine Junction and extends to Pine Point Mines, a distance of 54.3 miles. The entire route from Roma Junction (one mile from N. A. Rly Jct.) to Pine Junction to Pine Point is operated by Manual Block System. The only sections not under such operation are the 4 miles from Pine Point to Pine Point Mines and from Pine Junction to Hay River, a distance of 8.2 miles.

The railway has been built to high standards and includes hot box detectors at seven locations along the line, and can carry cars grossing out at 220,000 pounds. The highest train speed at this time is 30 miles per hour. Traffic in terms of number of trains is relatively light and rear end flag protection in accordance with Rule 99 is not yet required. This rule simply states that when a train stops for any reason out on the line, the rear end brakeman must go back about 2000 yards to flag down any following trains. However, with the Manual Block System only one train is permitted in a block at a time, and all train movements are under the direct supervision of the dispatcher. There are no passenger trains operated on the Great Slave Lake Railway.

The railway was built to open up a new territory in Canada. Although operated by the CN, the road carries its own name on locomotives with a slightly different color scheme. The territory served is just east of the Rockies, and therefore the weather is not as severe as it might otherwise be this far north. Therefore, farming is expanding throughout the area. In other words, the railway is pumping new life into a new territory, and this kind of expansion can only happen after a railway has been built. Civilization, as we know it, cannot come without the railway and that is a fact of geography. The Great Slave Lake Railway has a "Great" future ahead of it.

ONE OF THE biggest, if not the biggest, railway construction project in the 1960's was the Great Slave Lake Railway. It has been built to the highest standards including radio controlled main line trains. This photo shows an ore train with the engineer on the ground controlling the switching operation. Great Slave Lake and Canadian National units are operated together on the route.

Canadian National

THIS MAP SHOWS the route of the Great Slave Lake Railway from the Northern Alberta Railway connection to the Great Slave Lake.

Canadian National

GREAT SLAVE LAKE units, such as the 4341, are painted yellow with red ends and black lettering and underbody.

Canadian National

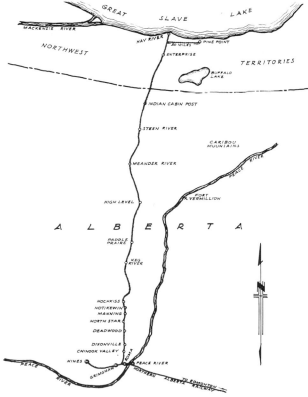

GREAT SLAVE LAKE RAILWAY
LENGTH 385 MILES.

DURING THE CONSTRUCTION DAYS, CN operated many ballast trains such as this one crossing the spectacular Meikle River Bridge. Note all of the units are in the old color scheme and the fourth unit is a switch engine MU'd with the three geeps.

Canadian National

CHAPTER 11

The Grand Trunk Western Railroad

The Grand Trunk Western Railroad is one of the more important railroads in the United States, and is part of the Montreal—Chicago main line. The railroad itself is actually the western end of the old Grand Trunk, and this is how the road got its name during the Canadian National amalgamation. As discussed earlier in this book, the U.S. lines of the Grand Trunk became separate companies, and all lines west of the Detroit River and Port Huron became the Grand Trunk Western. The GTW is not to be confused with the Grand Trunk Railway, the U.S. lines of Canadian National in New England, which in turn is not to be confused with the Central Vermont Railway.

The Grand Trunk Western is the largest of CN's rail subsidiaries. Its 951 mile route connects Port Huron and Detroit with Chicago plus a car ferry route from Muskegon, Michigan to Milwaukee, Wisconsin. All but 112 miles of GTW are located in the Wolverine State.

Historically GTW's operations have been closely related to Canadian National. A minimum of two freight trains have been operated daily in each direction between Chicago and Montreal, Quebec. One of these continues on to New England points, and this has been the case since the 1920's, both in steam and diesel. All through freight between Chicago or Milwaukee and Eastern Canada (east of Toronto) goes through Port Huron, while intermediate traffic destined or originated on lines to and from Windsor-Detroit goes through Detroit.

The GTW is sometimes known as the production line of the automobile manufacturers. Observing freights from the Detroit area, and also Lansing and Flint, reveals long strings of auto racks and auto parts cars in either regular freight trains, or sometimes solid trains for the auto industry. The Grand Trunk is the largest carrier of new automobiles in the State of Michigan. The new cars go in all directions to all parts of the USA and Canada, but they leave Michigan on the GTW.

Automobiles are not the only traffic on this fine railroad. Perishables from the west coast arrive in Chicago on the Santa Fe, Milwaukee Road and Chicago & North Western Railway. They are immediately interchanged with the GTW, and often dispatched east in solid trains.

Grand Trunk Western Railroad has always been maintained at high standards. Ever since the early 1950's, GTW freights have been authorized to operate at 60 miles per hour between Chicago and Port Huron, and Detroit. The only main line that is not block signal equipped, and without such high speed running is the route between Durand and Muskegon. This single track line, which ran to the car ferries across Lake Michigan, sports a 45 mph limit for freights and a 57 mph limit for passenger trains.

Traffic over the GTW has been relatively stable for a good many years since World War II. Normally there are about 12 freight trains in each direction between Durand and Chicago, except when the auto industry is at a low production level. When this happens traffic can fall to as few as six trains in each direction daily. Two of these are Chicago-Montreal runs, while two others operate on the Chicago-Detroit run. A fifth train operates as a way freight while still another serves as a drag freight picking up all other freight not handled by the speedsters.

An unusual part of GTW's service is the car ferry route between Muskegon, Michigan and Milwaukee, Wisconsin. This route adds Wisconsin to the states served by the GTW. The service is operated on a year around basis with the Madison and the Grand Rapids handling about 150 cars or more per day. These two car ferries were rebuilt in the mid-1960's to carry tri-level auto-rack cars and high cube box cars. Each ship can handle about 26 regular length freight cars, and can be loaded or unloaded in about 30 minutes. The average crossing time is about six hours.

GRAND TRUNK WESTERN No. 6407, a 4-8-4 Northern type, departs Pontiac, Michigan with white flags flying. The streamlined olive green locomotives were magnificent machines and the Vanderbilt tender only added to their beauty.
Bob Lorenz

Both ships have 16 passenger cabins, but do not handle automobiles, such as the Ann Arbor and C&O ferries did. They have ship to shore communications and radar. They also function as official United States weather stations and make regular reports on lake conditions. They carry 32 crewmen each.

The ferries have reinforced hulls as ice breakers and operate right through the winter, which is the peak season for GTW water traffic. During this time in years past, the City of Milwaukee, a third ferry, was delegated to the route. All ships are directed by the Marine Operations Department. However, in Feb., 1975, the GTW has petitioned the ICC to discontinue the car ferry service.

Passenger operations on the GTW have always been unusual when compared to other U.S. railroads. After the Grand Trunk amalgamation, GTW operated 5 passenger trains in each direction between Chicago and Port Huron. All were operated in conjunction with CN trains including the International Limited. Four long distance pas-senger trains in each direction operated in and out of Detroit. Of these only one was a Chicago train as such, while the others operated to and from Grand Rapids. Only one train operated beyond to Grand Haven, the terminal for the ferry operations during that time. Still another local passenger train operated between Muskegon, Greenville and Owosso and Durand. At that time the Greenville branch went all the way to Muskegon. Still other service operated between Pontiac and Caseville and a double daily between Durand and Bay City. The Depression struck, and passenger service was cut back. Further, the state of Michigan went all out for the construction of hard surfaced roads and the automobile made inroads on GTW passenger service in a much bigger and earlier invasion than in other states. World War II came and went, and GTW's passenger service before 1950 was substantially smaller. However, it had almost taken the form that it would continue for nearly 20 more years.

THE OLD AND the new paint schemes share the engine terminal in Chicago during April, 1969.

John H. Kuehl

GTW GP-18 NO. 4703 (class GR-18a) was one of 11 such units built by EMD in February and March of 1960. These were the latest GTW units to be painted in the green and yellow, and were the last to be purchased until 1969. The photo was taken at Elsdon yard in Chicago on November 7, 1970.

John H. Kuehl

OPERATING AS EXTRA 9026 East, four GTW "F" units move train No. 392 out of Elsdon yard with freight bound for Michigan and Eastern Canada. The date is September 5, 1970.

John H. Kuehl

ONE "COVERED WAGON" and two "geeps" power an eastbound freight from Pontiac to Detroit, and is shown here near Birmingham, Michigan on September 13, 1971.

Elmer Treloar

TWO GP-9's AND ONE GP-38 wheel an eastbound freight through Bloomfield Hills, Michigan. The third unit is painted blue instead of black.

Elmer Treloar

EASTBOUND GTW FREIGHT en route to Detroit rolls around the curve from the Chicago main line to the Detroit line behind two SD-40's at Durand.

Patrick C. Dorin

THREE D&TSL GEEPS power a westbound GTW freight through New Haven, Michigan en route from Port Huron to Detroit and Toledo, Ohio. D&TSL is partially owned by the GTW and the date of this photo is July 25, 1973. GTW diesel power is also found on D&TSL lines south of Detroit.

Elmer Treloar

NO. 21 EN ROUTE from Detroit to Muskegon as the Detroit-Muskegon Day Express steams through Bloomfield Hills, Michigan with four cars including a through coach for No. 17 at Durand for Chicago.

Elmer Treloar

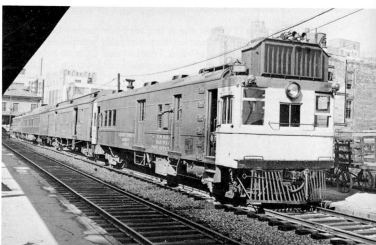

THE TRAIN WAS more famous than its power when photographed on a misty mid-day October, 1958 date in the pleasant surroundings of the Muskegon depot. Train 56 was the eastbound "side" of the last line haul steam powered passenger train in the United States: the afternoon cross Michigan service of GTW. The rear car was for the railway's medical examiner, and more head-end cars will be cut in at Grand Rapids. The coach was a heavyweight modernized with new non-reclining seats, better lighting and a largely maroon interior.

Jim Scribbins

TRAIN NO. 34 AWAITS its 3:15 PM departure time from Detroit for the 57 mile run to Port Huron. Running time was 1 hour, 55 minutes for the daily except Sunday run, while 35 departed Port Huron at 7:30 PM for a 9:20 PM arrival in the Motor City. The sleeper and coach behind the gas-electric's baggage car are part of No. 57's consist of the "Detroit-Muskegon Night Express."

Harold K. Vollrath Collection

P-5-g 0-8-0 No. 8373 pulls equipment for rush hour train No. 74 to a convenient spot along side the Pontiac platform. Use of the westbound track saves sleepy early risers the necessity of stepping over boardwalks. Shortly the k-4-a road engine will dig in and hustle through the crossover as the journey toward the Motor City commences. It is June, 1954.
Jim Scribbins

COMMUTER TRAIN NO. 79 departs the Brush Street Station in Detroit for Pontiac with streamlined steam power on June 4, 1959. It is the eve of dieselization for the GTW.

Elmer Treloar

GTW COMMUTER TRAINS today (1975), are equipped with former Union Pacific coaches and a single geep for power. The equipment is painted in the CN color scheme, which has been the custom for decades. This westbound train is crossing over the Chrysler Expressway in Detroit on August 19, 1971.

Elmer Treloar

THE GRAND TRUNK Western Railroad was a popular line among fans because of its longer use of steam power, and consequently several rail fan trips were operated over its lines. Here we seen an eastbound Michigan Railroad Club passenger extra east of Gaines, Michigan between Durand and Pontiac. The date is May 20, 1961.

Elmer Treloar

MANY FAN TRIPS included gondolas and cabooses for a few passengers to absorb the many sounds of railroading. The Greenville trip consisted of five coaches, one baggage recreation car, two more coaches, two gondolas and one caboose to hang the markers on.

C. A. Rogers & Sons Collection

144

NOT ALL GTW fan trips stuck to the main lines. Indeed some of the more interesting ones rolled down the branches to such places as Greenville, Michigan. Such a trip is shown here at Greenville in the early 1950's. Note the coaches have not been repainted green and black with the Maple Leafs.

C. A. Rogers & Sons Collection

GTW FREIGHT SERVICE GP-9 4139 lends a hand in moving an extremely long Maple Leaf out of Chicago during the Summer of 1967. Most of the passengers are en route to Expo '67 in Montreal.

John H. Kuehl

THREE CN "FP" units lead the eastbound Maple Leaf through Cassopolis, Michigan on May 17, 1969.

Sy Dykhouse

145

GP-9 NO. 4915 LEADS the coach only remnant of the once
lengthy and popular overnight "International Limited" into
Chicago on a dark and dreary April 16, 1971. The train had
been cut back to a Chicago-Port Huron operation.

John H. Kuehl

GTW PASSENGER TRAIN No. 168 awaits passengers from
train No. 158 (the Maple Leaf) before departing for Detroit from
Durand. April, 1971.

Patrick C. Dorin

GRAND TRUNK WESTERN train No. 158, the Toronto bound
Maple Leaf pauses at Durand to load passengers for Canadian
points, and to unload passengers for Detroit train No. 168. The
consist of the train was usually two geeps, one baggage car,
three coaches and dining parlor car (either Silver Lake or
Diamond Lake).

Patrick C. Dorin, April, 1971

THE DINING PARLOR cars Silver Lake and Diamond Lake
operated in both the Maple Leaf and the Mohawk during their
careers on the GTW. The cars were later designated club-diner
lounge cars.

Bill Raia

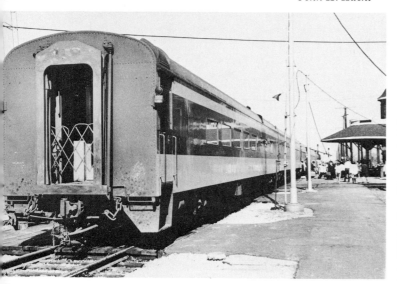

THE INTERIOR OF the dining room of the Silver Lake.

Canadian National

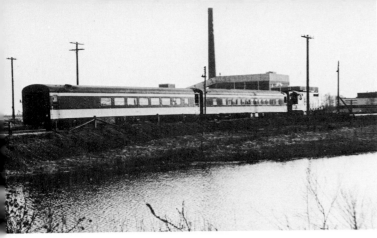

IT IS APRIL 27, 1971 and in three more days, GTW No. 165, the Mohawk, will succumb to Amtrak. The usual consist for the Detroit-Chicago speedster was a single GP-9, a leg rest coach and a food bar coach. However, weekends and holiday travel often expanded the train to seven cars—still with one geep.
Patrick C. Dorin

EXPRESS CAR 8805 in the mid-fifties colors; at Dearborn Station, Chicago, October, 1964. Actually, as can be determined by the placard, the car was being used in "storage" mail service.
Jim Scribbins

GTW PASSENGER COACH No. 4887 built by Pullman Standard in 1953. Note the vestibule at each end of the car.
Patrick C. Dorin

GTW SEMI-STREAMLINED heavyweight coach No. 5320.
Patrick C. Dorin

GTW DID A fine job of upgrading heavyweight coaches, such as the 5325, into a semi-streamlined vehicle for daytime service. Interior was basically maroon, and the Canadian principle of dividing the non-recliner into non-smoking and smoking sections was maintained.
Jim Scribbins

COACH NO. 5333 in the mid-1950's green and black livery which was adopted at the CN's large post war order of streamlined equipment was delivered.
Jim Scribbins

COACH NO. 5318 indicates how standard era cars could be upgraded into quite attractive vehicles for the 1950's with reclining seats and lowered ceilings and improved lighting. This shows clearly the creditable "Canadian" practice of maintaining a separate portion of each coach for smokers rather than the usual US style smoking rooms.

Jim Scribbins

THE NEWEST MOTIVE power as of early 1975 were the blue, red-orange and white GP-38's. The units carry the new blue color scheme, and mark for the first time in history that GTW's color arrangement differed from parent Canadian National.

Bill Raia

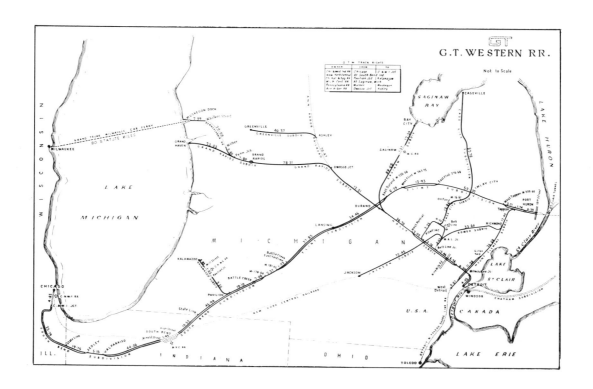

CHAPTER 12

The Grand Trunk Railway

Of all the Canadian National railway subsidiaries, the Grand Trunk Railway could be called the "one that isn't." The present status of the Grand Trunk is a small segment of railroad line making up the Berlin Subdivision of the Champlain Area. The Berlin Sub extends from Island Pond, Vermont to Portland, Maine, a distance of 149.5 miles. This is all that exists in 1975 of the once proud Grand Trunk Railway empire.

With the take over of the Grand Trunk by Canadian National, all lines went into CNR operation with the exception of this segment of railway. Indeed, this segment also went under CN operating procedures but retained the name Grand Trunk Railway for legal purposes. Further locomotives and cabooses retained Grand Trunk insignias. As stated previously in Chapter 10, to distinguish between the geographic territories of Grand Trunk properties in the United States, the lines in Michigan, Indiana, Illinois and Wisconsin were named Grand Trunk Western; while the New England carrier simply retained the name Grand Trunk.

The line originated as the Atlantic and St. Lawrence Railroad in 1852. The company operated independently until 1898 when the Grand Trunk Railway gained control. From that time on, the A & StL was owned and operated by Grand Trunk until financial collapse changed the entire picture.

Steam motive power did not change drastically on the GT after the CN takeover. A number of engines assigned to the property carried GT identification instead of Canadian National lettering. However most of these, if not all, were of CNR ownership and there was no distinction in number series. Indeed, many locomotives flowed freely back and forth between New England and Canada if they met Interstate Commerce Commission rules, regulations and standards. Otherwise CN engines were permitted to stay only 24 hours in the States.

With diesel power the situation was somewhat different. Basically four sets of diesel locomotives were purchased by Canadian National for Grand Trunk service, and these engines carried Grand Trunk lettering on their hoods.

The first pair of engines were built by Alco in 1954. Road switcher type RS-3, CN road class MR–16d, the pair was originally numbered 1861 and 1862. However, they were renumbered 3041 and 3042 in 1956 and reassigned to the Canadian National.

The year 1956 brought a brace of GP–9's from EMD that are now numbered 4442 to 4450 and 4902 to 4906 (originally 1768 to 1776 and 1777 to 1781 respectively). The following year brought another pair of GP–9's, 4558 and 4559. The tiny property had the distinction of being completely dieselized with a grand total of 16 GP–9's. However, as one might guess, the GP–9's didn't always stay at home. They often roam far and wide showing up on the Central Vermont, Grand Trunk Western and the Duluth, Winnipeg and Pacific as well as CN freight and/or passenger service east and west of the Great Lakes.

Passenger service after Canadian National control consisted of two passenger trains daily each way between Portland, Maine and Montreal. There was a pair of overnight trains numbered 34 and 14, and 15 and 33. (On the GT section the trains were 14 and 15.) In addition to mail, baggage and express traffic, the trains carried through coaches, and a single standard section sleeper. A cafe parlor car was operated between Island Pond and Portland. Eastbound No. 14 was allowed 20 minutes to add the car at 4:50 AM, but 15 was permitted only 10 minutes at 10:55 PM in the evening. No. 14 arrived in Portland at 11:00 AM after a 12 hour, 20 minute schedule for the 297 mile run. No. 15 departed Portland at 5:00 PM and was scheduled for 13 hours, 25 minutes for its westbound run.

GRAND TRUNK RAILWAY 2-8-0 No. 2612 steams softly before leaving Portland with an extra west in March, 1956.
Harold K. Vollrath Collection

GRAND TRUNK RAILWAY 2-8-0's roamed far and wide from home territory. Here we see the 2575 in switching service at the West Virginia, Minnesota yard of the Duluth, Winnipeg and Pacific Railway in August, 1955.
Harold K. Vollrath Collection

GRAND TRUNK RAILWAY passenger GP-9 No. 4905 was one of five such units (4902 to 4906) operated for both freight and passenger service not only on the Grand Trunk, but also Central Vermont and Grand Trunk Western. GT geeps often showed up on the DW&P in Minnesota. The photo was taken in July, 1963 at Portland, Maine.
Harold K. Vollrath Collection

WITH ONLY THE GT symbol on both Grand Trunk and Grand Trunk Western equipment, it is often difficult for one to determine if a car or locomotive is GT or GTW unless the numbering system is known. This caboose, No. 77971, is a Grand Trunk Railway caboose in service at Portland, Maine in June, 1965.
Harold K. Vollrath Collection

JOINT GRAND TRUNK-Canadian National weekend passenger special prepares to depart Portland for Montreal with a seven car train including six coaches. This weekend special was the last regular passenger service over the Grand Trunk. The photo was taken on August 15, 1962.

J. W. Swanberg

CHAPTER 13

Central Vermont Railway

As stated previously with the Grand Trunk Western, the Central Vermont is deserving of a book all by itself. With its Canadian influence, Central Vermont was and is one of the more colorful roads of New England. The railway can trace its beginnings back to 1835, long before any thought would be given to the railway being part of the Canadian National Railways.

The original charter granted by the State of Vermont to the "Vermont Central" expired in 1835, but a second charter was granted on Oct. 31, 1843 for the railway to Charles Paine, the first president of the new railroad, However, as usual, it took 10 years before ground was broken on December 15, 1845 at Windsor, Vermont. During the next four years construction was slow, but the first segment was completed from Windsor to Burlington in 1849. During the first fiscal year of operation, ending June 30, 1849, the new road carried 47,000 passengers and 25,000 tons of freight.

In 1855 the first step of Canadian influence took place when the Vermont Central was purchased by the Vermont & Canada. This provided a through operation to Montreal. In 1860, the headquarters of the Vermont Central was moved from Northfield to St. Albans. From that time through 1873 the Vermont Central expanded its system from Canada to the Atlantic Ocean at New London, Conn. They also had leased the Rutland Railway and several other smaller railroads to form a system over 900 miles long. They also owned the Ogdensburgh Transit Line which provided water connection with eight steamers to Detroit, Chicago, Milwaukee and other Great Lakes ports.

In 1873 the name of the Vermont Central was changed to the Central Vermont Railroad. Shortly after that financial conditions changed and the CV released control of the Rutland Railroad, the Vermont Valley, the Sullivan County line and the Ogdensburgh Branch. The Central Vermont became only a fraction of its former system, and in 1896 the road went into receivership. During the

next two years, the Grand Trunk Railway acquired the controlling stock interest with the financial arrangements that bailed the railroad out of trouble.

Things went smoothly during the next few years, and there were no significant changes during the Grand Trunk's amalgamation with Canadian National. The Central Vermont Railroad retained its own separate identity, which it still does to this day.

In 1927 trouble sprang up again and massive floods wiped out the railroad between Essex Junction and White River Junction. The CV slipped into bankruptcy with the disaster. However, rebuilding had to be done, and the Canadian National loaned the CV $3 million for the reconstruction project which took three months to complete. Part of the loan was used to reorganize the CV which subsequently emerged as Central Vermont Railway, Inc., which is the present company. The CV currently operates 375 miles of railroad from New London to East Alburgh, Vermont, its connection with Canadian National. This mileage includes two branches to Burlington, Vermont; and Richford, Vermont.

The Central Vermont has been highly important to the economy of the state of Vermont. This was widely recognized in the late 1920's, when every year the CV operated a "Vermont Special" with a delegation of leading business and professional men and women of the state. The train toured the south and mid-west, usually over a ten day period of time and stopping at as many cities as possible on the approximate 4000 mile annual excursion. Central Vermont was commissioned to manage the transportation and assembled 14 car trains which included at least five baggage cars filled with Vermont's natural and manufactured products. The trains always originated, appropriately enough, at the state capital Montpelier. There have been few operations of this sort on any railroad.

ST. ALBANS, VERMONT is the general headquartesr for the Central Vermont Railway, and the facility included a four track train shed. The entire complex was at one time very unusual among railroad stations in Canada and the United States.

Harold K. Vollrath Collection

Prior to the Depression, Central Vermont operated three name trains in each direction every day. Trains 20 and 21, the Washingtonian and the Montrealer, respectively, carried a full complement of coaches, dining cars and sleepers between Montreal, New York City and Washington. The train also carried through sleepers between Ottawa and New York and Quebec and Washington.

The New Englander was the night train between Montreal and Boston and Springfield. This train too carried sleepers and coaches between all points as well as club car service between Boston and Montreal.

The day schedule was the Ambassador between Montreal and Boston. She carried the finest of observation parlor cars, buffet parlor car, dining car and coaches. The train was advertised as the fastest between Boston and Montreal with no excess fare. All of CV's passenger operations were in joint service with Canadian National and the Boston & Maine, except of course the branch line services to Burlington, Vermont.

The Depression didn't play any favorites, and Central Vermont was no exception. On February 1, 1932, the Burlington branch passenger service was replaced by bus service for coach passengers, and limousine service for Pullman passengers.

The highway connecting runs provided a direct trainside connection at Essex Junction. Mail, express and baggage service was provided by trucks that also made direct trainside connections.

However, the Depression did not throw the Central Vermont into a complete tail spin. A positive attitude was maintained, and the road was constantly looking for ways to improve service and reduce expenses. From 1935 on, things were definitely on the upswing. In fact, a new era was introduced in rail coach service on June 23, 1935.

On that date, the Ambassador became the first day coach train to carry a club–lounge car for coach passengers in the USA. Further the train schedule was reduced by 1 hour, 45 minutes in both directions. The new schedule departed Boston at noon and arrived at Montreal at 8:15 PM. Southbound departure was 11:00 AM with arrival in Boston at 7:15 PM. This new scheduled permitted businessmen to have a full morning in either Boston or Montreal and yet be at their destination that evening. The new schedule also provided a fast early afternoon service for Bostonians traveling to vacation centers in Vermont.

The club lounge car featured 39 individual chairs and two divans with a full porter service. All coaches on the train were air conditioned, and the train was truly a fine train for 1935. The old schedules departed Boston and Montreal at 8:00 AM and 8:40 AM respectively.

The Central Vermont was also extensively involved in snow trains or ski trains to and from the Vermont ski resorts during the late 1930's. CV issued a winter sports booklet entitled "When the Green Mountains Turn White." Its contents included half tone reproductions of action and scenic pictures made in the snow country of Mt. Mansfield, Vermont and complete train and plane schedules. CV carried ski parties on both regular and special trains operated in conjunction with the B&M, New Haven and Pennsylvania Railroads.

The Depression and World War II did not break up CV's passenger service too badly. The motor train still operated between Brattleboro, Vermont and New London, Conn. The New Englander was combined with the Montrealer and Washingtonian, and the Ambassador continued on their daily assignments. There was a new train, The Vermonter, which more or less replaced the New Englander's schedule between St. Albans and White River Junction. This train provided an overnight sleeping car service between St. Albans and New York, and the sleeper and head-end cars were handled in the Montrealer and Washingtonian between White River Junction and New York. One other change included the handling of thru day time service (coaches only) between Montreal and New York on the Ambassador. This equipment was handled in Boston & Maine and New Haven trains south of White River Junction.

For the next fifteen years to 1960, the train schedules remained pretty much intact. The New London–Brattleboro motor train was dropped by the early 1950's.

However, the Ambassador became a Rail Diesel Car operation with through RDC's running between Montreal-Boston and Montreal-Springfield. Passengers destined to New York City changed trains at Springfield. The Vermonter became a simple local train without its through sleeping car to New York. The train still departed St. Albans late in the evening and made a turn about run to White River Junction arriving there at 12:25 AM. It departed northbound at 2:30 AM arriving at St. Albans at 6:00 AM. Its sole purpose by this time was to simply relieve the Montrealer and Washingtonian of head-end traffic and burdensome local stops.

THE HEAVY STEAM power on the CV was the 700 series 2-10-4's. In this photo the 709 has stretched the slack on 63 cars on time freight No. 491 departing St. Albans, Vermont on May 10, 1952.

George-Paterson Collection

NO. 468, A 2-8-0, powers train No. 814 through Milton, Vermont en route to White River Junction on May 1, 1954. Note the single milk car on the head-end of the local.

George-Paterson Collection

By 1964, through RDC service was dropped on the Ambassador between Montreal and Boston. The B&M continued to operate RDC's to and from White River Junction, but the CN–CV elected to run through coaches between Montreal and New York. The Ambassador had become a through Montreal–New York train, somewhat different than its original run between Montreal–Boston.

By 1966, the Vermonter had been dropped as well as the B&M's connecting run to and from Boston for the Ambassador. Only the Washingtonian and the Montrealer, trains 20 and 21 carried on in the fine tradition. The train was streamlined and carried through Montreal–New York coaches (as she always did), a 14 roomette, 4 double bedroom sleeper between Montreal and Washington; a 6 section, 6 roomette, 4 double bedroom sleeper Montreal–New York and a 6 double bedroom, buffet lounge car between Montreal–New York. All Central Vermont passenger service was discontinued in 1966.

However, there is a happy postscript to the discontinuance of passenger service on the Central Vermont. In 1973, Amtrak, Central Vermont and Canadian National teamed up to put the Montrealer back in service between Washington and Montreal. The train is scheduled so that skiers may get off the train near ski resorts early in the

morning, such as Waterbury, and offers more services than ever before. In addition to complete dining and beverage service in the dining car, the new all-reserved train offers light meal and beverage service in the Pub/lounge car. Sleeping car passengers may be served in their room upon request.

Beside the usual coach and sleeping car service between Montreal and Washington, the new train offers a Montreal–Miami through sleeping car operation. Coach passengers receive complimentary pillows and blankets for the overnight trip, and everybody receives complimentary wake-up coffee and orange juice during the hours from 6:00 AM to 9:00 AM. It is good to see the Montrealer back in service after so many years of absence.

Freight service on the Central Vermont has not taken a back seat to any railroad. It is sometimes said that necessity is the mother of invention and in the case of the CV, the Depression sired its "Rocket" freight service.

The original term "Rocket" was applied to a fast merchandise train operated in conjunction with the Boston & Maine from Boston to St. Albans on an overnight schedule. The new high speed service began early in the Depression, and later the term "Rocket" was applied to all of the CV's fast merchandise service. (The term died away altogether as the Rock Island Railroad picked it up for its new streamliners during the latter part of the Depression.)

The Central Vermont has been a pioneer in new operating techniques in freight service. For example, it began pickup and delivery service on July 4, 1932. This later expanded to a complete highway service covering the entire railroad, which in turn provided a more prompt and more flexible merchandise handling. It is interesting to note that before a truck route was set up, the local shippers were consulted as to their needs. The local sales practices and the schedules of the traveling salesmen were carefully studied and the service placed on the basis of what the shipper really wanted and could get from highway truck operators.

The next step after the study was to paint each Central Vermont caboose as a rolling advertisement of Rocket freight service, and the local newspapers and radio stations were used for other advertising. Then every CV employee who could be spared from his regular duties was given a portion of the territory to cover during a week's campaign. Advertising flyers were then distributed to every shipper and receiver in the territory.

The trucks, too, were painted to advertise Rocket service. Truck operators and drivers and all railway men attended monthly meetings held by the traffic department to discuss progress and problems as they occurred. The result was that a previous steady decline in traffic was halted and merchandise came back to the railroad.

Prior to World War II, the CV provided an overnight service between New York and points in Connecticut and Massachusetts as far north as Brattleboro, Vermont. The merchandise was handled by Central Vermont Transportation Company steamships between New York and New London, Connecticut, a distance of 125 miles through Long Island Sound. From New London, the freight moved by a combination of a fast mixed merchandise, express, passenger train and highway trucks between New London and Brattleboro, the rail distance being 121 miles.

The train operation was originally a rail motor car which ran from New London to Brattleboro in the morning and returned in the afternoon. (This motor car went back into service during the War.) It was necessary to run this train for a variety of reasons, and it ran at a loss until its potentialities as an adjunct to Rocket freight service were discovered. After an experimental period when a number of freight shipments were made in the baggage compartment of the motor car, it was determined that the new fast freight service could be operated successfully. However, the volume of merchandise traffic dictated that the motor car train be replaced by a steam train handling the limited amount of mail, express and passengers, but primarily for handling the merchandise freight shipments. Baggage cars were re-equipped for the new service and the operation included several set out cars for various collection and distribution points. The baggage cars were distinctively painted and lettered for the Rocket service.

Central Vermont employed cartage agents in New York City who trucked the freight to and from New York receivers and shippers and the pier. The freight was loaded on special trailers at the piers in New York and New London and the ships were equipped with side hatchways for loading and unloading these trailers by a donkey engine. The use of the trailers provided a safe and convenient transport by water, and for efficient transfer between ship and motor trucks and/or rail cars at the piers.

The northbound train departed New London at 4:45 AM and after serving the intermediate points arrived in Brattleboro at 10:05 AM. Returning, it departed Brattleboro at 3:30 PM and arrived in New London at 8:42 PM, thereby giving the ship plenty of time to arrive in New York the following morning, so that the cartage agents could make their deliveries before 9:00 AM.

Between New London and Brattleboro the intermediate stations for both pick up and delivery and interstation movements were served by numerous truck lines, which took the freight from

CV EMPLOYED HEAVY 0-8-0's, like the 507, in yard service at St. Albans, Vermont. The photo was taken in September, 1947.

Harold K. Vollrath Collection

CV 0-6-0 SWITCHER NO. 387 works quietly around the yards at St. Johnsburg, Vermont in July, 1937.

Harold K. Vollrath Collection

WITH THREE MILK cars on the head-end, 2-8-0 No. 469 zips along with the 10 car consist of way freight No. 210 near St. Albans, Vermont on May 10, 1952.

George-Paterson Collection

and to the distribution and collection points where cars are set out by the train. The highway equipment was also brightly painted and lettered to advertise Rocket service.

The rail route between Brattleboro and Windsor is owned by the Boston and Maine, with CV having trackage rights. However, no local freight service was or is provided by the CV between these points.

However, from Windsor north to the Canadian border, a system of rail-highway coordination was in effect similar to that on the south end of the CV. Second morning delivery service from New York City and overnight service to and from Boston in connection with the B&M via White River Junction was in operation.

World War II disrupted the operating techniques of this service through no fault of the CV.

After the war, CV no longer opeated the steam ships between New London and New York City upon working out an agreement for the interchange of freight traffic with the New Haven. The Rocket freight service, as such, was phased out.

For decades however, the principal freight of the CV consisted of imports and exports to and from all points in Canada through the ports of New London, Boston, Providence and New York City. The other source of traffic was and is freight routed between New England points and Chicago–Milwaukee and points west via Montreal and the Boston & Maine, Canadian National and Grand Trunk Western Railways. The four railways participate in the operation of "second morning delivery" freight service in both directions. As far as the CV's main line is concerned, there are two freight trains in each direction south of White

158

River Junction, and three in each direction north of that point. A deep water pier is maintained at the port of New London.

CV motive power, both steam and diesel, has ventured off line not only to the Canadian National, but also to the Grand Trunk, Grand Trunk Western and the Duluth, Winnipeg & Pacific.

At the present time Central Vermont is operated as a separate railway but as part of the St. Lawrence Region's Champlain Area.

The Central Vermont Railway can be summed up as an interesting little railroad. Since it handles only about 2.5 million tons of freight annually, it does not compare to a road like the heavy tonnage Bessemer & Lake Erie Railroad. However, it will be long remembered for its superb 2–10–4's (700 series) and the 4–8–2 Mountains in the 600 series. The road also operated 8 fine 0–8–0's (500 series) for switching at St. Albans. The Central Vermont is an essential part of the New England economy, and the railway has performed an outstanding service over the past decades.

A CENTRAL VERMONT passenger train prepares to depart from the old St. Bonaventure Station in Montreal on June 14, 1938.

George-Paterson Collection

TRAIN NO. 332, the southbound Ambassador, passes St. Lambert, Quebec on February 29, 1952. Note the milk car on the head-end. Milk traffic was once very important for the Central Vermont, and such equipment could be found in the consist of both freight and passenger trains.

George-Paterson Collection

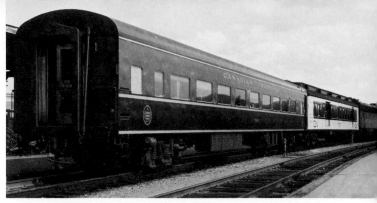

IT IS TWO years later, and the consist of the Ambassador has changed somewhat. The RPO-Baggage is marked "Canadian National" but includes the wording "United States Railway Post Office." The consist includes a Cafe Grill car, and two coaches.

George-Paterson Collection

TECHNICALLY A BOSTON & Maine train, now that the red and gold F units have been attached, the southbound Ambassador waits at White River Junction, Vermont to continue its Montreal-New York run. Both "sides" of this international train met at White River Jct., and the geep which brought this train from Montreal returned immediately on the northbound train. In May, 1963, the CN's new image was just commencing and the head-end car has a distinctive treatment of its black center stripe.

Jim Scribbins

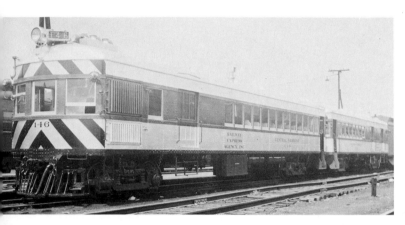

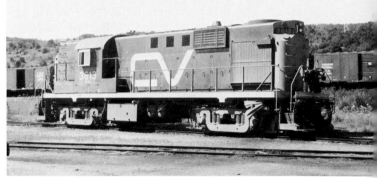

CENTRAL VERMONT INVESTED in two combination coach-baggage gas electric cars. The two cars are shown here at Montreal on June 28, 1936.

George-Paterson Collection

THE DW&P LOANED several 1800 HP Alco RS-11's to the Central Vermont in the 1960's. Around 1968, the units returned to the Northern Minnesota carrier but retained the CV markings for quite some time. This unit is shown here at the DW&P's West Duluth round house.

Patrick C. Dorin

WHAT APPEARS TO be a Central Vermont SW1200, the 1502 is actually a GTW unit which was assigned to the CV from the mid-1950's through 1968. The GTW did not reletter the unit until mid-1972. The trucks on this unit are EMD's Pioneer "Re-Flexicoils," which were rebuilt from standard type AAR-A trucks.

John H. Kuehl

AMONG THE VARIOUS locomotives purchased for the dieselization process were five GP-9's (4547 to 4551) which were part of a larger order of about 33 geeps including 12 for passenger service. Some of these units have been transferred to other parts of the system and no longer operate on a regular basis on the Central Vermont. This photo shows one of the GP-9's in the original color scheme.

Canadian National

THERE WERE TWO Alco RS-3's with steam generators built for the CV in 1954. They were later renumbered 3900-3901 (CN road class MRG-16c) and reassigned to Canadian National. This photo shows the 1860 prior to renumbering leading milk train No. 814 near Milton, Vermont on April 22, 1955.
George-Paterson Collection

CV CABOOSE NO. 4022 was typical of the three window wood cabooses operated by that railway. This caboose is bringing up the rear of a freight that has just crossed the Boston & Albany tracks at Palmer, Mass.

J. W. Swanberg

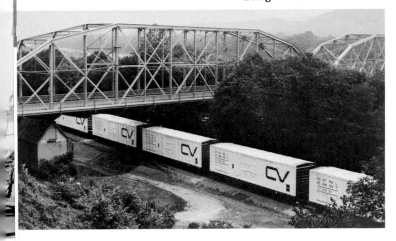

DURING 1974 CENTRAL VERMONT took delivery of 100 new box cars. They are 50 feet long, with 100 ton capacity, 10 foot plug doors and equipped with cushion underframes. The last five cars were painted a bright white with Kelly green lettering and black underframes, ends and trucks. The purpose of the distinctive color scheme was to focus on the local nature of the CV in its own region. All 100 cars are used primarily in international newsprint service.

Canadian National

WHEN AMTRAK PROPOSED service for the Central Vermont, the people in Vermont were most enthusiastic. The result was that volunteers, with the help of Amtrak, refurbished several of the ruggedly handsome passenger stations along the Central Vermont's route of the "Montrealer." Volunteers are shown here working on Montpelier Junction, Vermont depot.

Amtrak

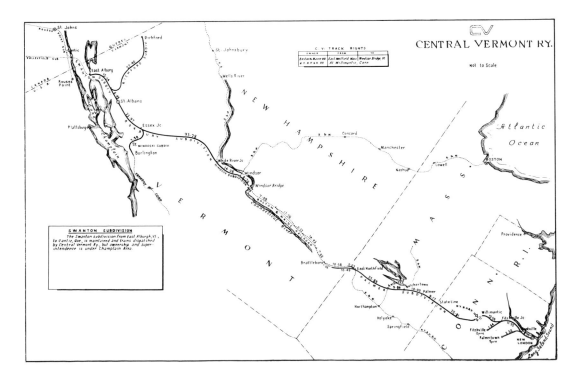

AS OF EARLY 1975, many DW&P units are receiving a modified color scheme with large white safety stripes and a complete orange red cab.

Canadian National

DULUTH, WINNIPEG & PACIFIC Railway train No. 732 arrives at West Duluth yard on a beautiful summer morning in 1969. The two units, although painted Central Vermont, are actually DW&P units which had been loaned earlier to the New England carrier.

Patrick C. Dorin

EXTRA 3609 NORTH, complete with white flags, gurgles out of West Virginia yard with two DW&P Alcos and two CN geeps and 88 cars. This April, 1974 day is foggy in Northern Minnesota and snow is forcasted further north. This particular train ran with just the two CN units from West Duluth, and has now picked up two additional units for the final leg of the trip to Fort Frances over the Cusson Subdivision. All northward trains operate as extras.

Patrick C. Dorin

CANADIAN NATIONAL CABOOSES run through from Winnipeg to Duluth and return. CN 79545, stenciled for international service, carries the markers for Extra 3609 North.

Patrick C. Dorin

FIRST 792, COMPLETE with green flags, arrives at West Virginia yard with 88 cars. The two lead units will cut off and the entire train, without any switching at this yard, will continue onto the Rices Point Yard in Duluth after changing crews. This train was blocked at Symington Yard in Winnipeg for the Burlington Northern. The date is April 13, 1974.

Patrick C. Dorin

FIRST 792 HOLDS THE main line at West Virginia, but cabooses are no longer changed at this division point as they once were. The train has just left the Cusson Subdivision, and will roll south to Duluth over the Taft Subdivision. With no cabooses to change or cars to block, the switch crew stands idle until the hot shot freight departs. She will run as First 732 to Duluth. The second section was one hour behind on this Saturday morning.

Patrick C. Dorin

DW&P TRAIN NO. 417 running as Extra 4304 North drums across a bridge just north of West Duluth in August, 1974. The consist on this cold and rainy day included but 4 loads and 79 empties for a total of 2,794 tons. No. 417 is a thru Chicago-Winnipeg run via the Chicago & North Western, DW&P and CN Railways.

Patrick C. Dorin

FREIGHT EN ROUTE to Chicago & North Western Railway destinations and beyond does not wait long at the Duluth interchange with the DW&P. This particular train arrived in Duluth at 7:00 AM and had been totally blocked at the Symington yard in Winnipeg. Upon arrival at Duluth, the C&NW's transfer crew brought the entire train to the Superior, Wisconsin Itasca Yard. By 10:30 AM the train was rolling in Extra 6850 South en route to Milwaukee where the first switching would take place. Note that the entire consist of the train appears to be almost exclusively Canadian National box cars on the head-end of the train. The total consist included 110 cars and two helper engines on the rear end. It was a very cold (10 below zero) March 23, 1974.

Patrick C. Dorin

WOODEN CABOOSE NO. 79159 carries the markers for symbol freight No. 884 running as train No. 732 over the Taft Subdivision from West Virginia yard to West Duluth yard. 884 is a drag freight from Fort Frances, Ontario to Duluth and carries non-rush freight. For example the gondola ahead of the caboose is loaded with zinc ore. The consist included 105 loads, 7 empties for 10,410 tons. In contrast to 417, symbol 884 was powered by three DW&P RS-11's 3608, 3614 and 3602. The photo was taken at West Virginia yard on August 2, 1974.

Patrick C. Dorin

SYMBOL FREIGHT 884 (No. 732) meets No. 883 running as Extra 3603 North at Melrude at 5:30 PM on August 2, 1974. 883 is in the 85 car siding as 884 highballs down the main line en route to West Duluth. The covered hoppers on the head-end of 883 will be set out at the Ford Fairlane Taconite Plant. The C&NW cars contain bentonite clay from South Dakota which is used to bind the taconite pellets.

Patrick C. Dorin

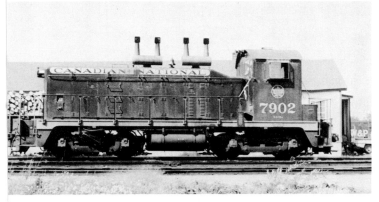

THE DW&P OFTEN assigns a CN switch engine to yard service at the West Virginia yard. The photo was taken in August, 1972.

Patrick C. Dorin

DURING THE PAST few years, the DW&P has often been short of motive power. To aleviate such shortages the DW&P has often leased power from its neighbor, the Duluth, Missabe and Iron Range Railway. SD-9 units 144 and 142 are being readied for an extra north in December, 1973. The location is the West Duluth round house.

Patrick C. Dorin

CHAPTER 15

Research and Development

No book about the Canadian National would be complete without a look at the Research and Development Department. Originally called the Bureau of Economics, because then, as now, cost research, financial analysis and point-to-point cost estimating were an integral and most necessary part of railway operations, the Research and Development title was adopted in 1939.

In addition to the costing services section, which provides Marketing functions with estimates of the variable costs of rail transportation or competitive modes, keeps abreast of developments in other transportation areas and provides analytical statements for management information and direction, there are four other distinct sections.

They are: operational research, strategic projects, industrial engineering and loss and damage prevention. Leaving operational research until later because of its complexities and detailed story, the remaining three units can be described as follows:

Strategic projects tackles development activities and the assignments may vary in length of completion from a few days to a year or two. The work consists as much in identifying critical problem areas as in designing an approach for their solution. Some recent endeavors have included evaluating potential developments in the Canadian north, acquisition studies and supporting other departments and CN subsidiaries.

Industrial engineering specializes in increasing productivity of men and equipment, making materials handling studies, designing and development of tools and techniques and setting up car control systems, reservation systems, tie renewal charts, and countless other efforts. Loss and damage prevention means just what it says, a specific unit which identifies commodities prone to loss and damage in rail transportation, establish causes and determine the remedy whether it means talking to a railroad department or a particular customer.

Now on to operational research which supports management through improvements in rail per-

formance and planning and decision making for capital investment; development of new techniques for solving problems and development of long range operational plans. Some of the recent projects include a network model using a computer to simulate car movement in trains and through yards; diesel fleet planning based on performance evaluation; the design; development and implementation of a traffic reporting and control system (TRACS) to improve car utilization, and a newsprint distribution study aimed at reducing distribution costs of Canadian newsprint to U.S. markets.

Meanwhile in technical research, CN has the only intermodal research center in North America. Although CN made use of various research techniques for decades, the late 1940's and 50's saw much of the operation devoted to testing and quality control. Today, however, the CN technical research Centre, which opened in December, 1964, is doing 90% research.

The scope of the Centre's activities are limitless, and have benefitted not only CN but railways in general and industry throughout the world. It is interesting to note that a number of research projects have been patented by CN and sold to industry under licensing agreements. Very few corporation research centers can point to such achievements.

The Canadian National's Technical Research Centre is today (1975) one of the most modern railway research establishments in the world, and is the largest centre in Canada. The 8½ acres site is made up of a 42,000 square foot main research building, a locomotive and car research building and an "inclined" impact track.

The Centre's professional staffs hold doctorates, masters and bachelor degrees in nearly all of the branches of the physical sciences and engineering disciplines. They complete, on the average, about 500 research projects annually.

They work with the most modern equipment available and in addition to the normal research instrumentation this equipment includes:

THE AUTOMATIC JOURNAL oiler squirts a jet spray of oil into a journal box of a box car.
Canadian National

1. A "hot" room for research on insulated and refrigerated equipment and on environmental control.
2. Analog and digital computers for data analysis.
3. Dynamometers, transducers and specialized recording equipment for dynamic and stress analysis.
4. Infra-red spectroscopic equipment.
5. Gas chromatographic equipment.
6. Atomic absorption spectrographic equipment.
7. Specialized equipment for textile research.
8. An electron probe microscope.
9. A fully instrumented research car for over the road measurement of train dynamics.
10. A special computer for random vibration research and power spectral density analysis.
11. A specialized computer centre to advance the development of various simulations required to solve complex railway engineering problems.
12. A "cold" room for low temperature research.

The work of the Centre serves the entire Canadian National system including the rail, road and water transportation as well as hotel and telecommunications. The overall goal is to increase the safety and efficiency of all CN services and to reduce operating costs through the improvement to productivity.

To accomplish this all activities have been broken down into three major divisions: engineering research, materials and processes research and inspection and quality control services. The rest of this chapter describes some of the projects and accomplishments of the Research Centre.

AUTOMATIC JOURNAL OILER

Although automatic journal oilers are not exactly new, CN's oiler has a new and different twist. Operation begins at the receiving yards where car men open all journal boxes requiring lubrication. As the cars move by the oiler, the open boxes are detected by a sensing device which activates the oiler. Contact of the freight car wheel on a roller device moves the oiler platform along at the same speed as the moving freight cars In other words, the oiler moves with the car.

The platform's forward motion causes the oiling arm to be lowered to a vertical position, a switch is closed and the oil begins to flow. A timing device stops the flow after eight ounces have been pumped into the journal box. Air is mixed with the oil at the nozzle to prevent splash back or waste of oil. The in-motion journal oiler is now manufactured and marketed by Ramsey REC Ltd of Richmond Hill, Ontario.

ELECTRONIC SCALE FOR WEIGHING RAILWAY CARS

One of the first significant developments of the Technical Research Centre was the electronic scale for weighing moving cars. Again such a concept is not new, but this particular scale is able to weigh cars with weights up to 500,000 pounds at speeds up to 15 miles per hour. This innovation has enabled CN to cut up to 24 hours from delivery times of shipments. CN also awarded the worldwide rights for manufacturing and marketing of this scale to Ramsey REC Limited.

A BALTIMORE & OHIO coal hopper moves over the electronic scale for weighing moving cars at the Montreal Yard.
Canadian National

ANALOG LOCOMOTIVE SPEEDOMETER

This speedometer was developed in 1965 for use on locomotives and rapid transit vehicles. This innovation is designed to withstand the extreme vibration common with locomotives and eliminate the most common causes of misinterpretation found in other speed indicators, i.e., distortion, needle fluctuation and unclear readout.

The speedometer provides precise low speed indication in tenths of a mile per hour for speeds up to 10 miles per hour, and accurate speed in miles per hour up to 199 mph. The license for the marketing and manufacture of this device has been sold by Canadian National to Vapor Canada Limited.

TRACK RECORDER CAR

The track recorder car is capable of measuring and evaluating the surface condition of track at speeds up to 100 miles per hour. The car is a converted passenger coach filled with sophisticated computers. Yet the car is unique in its simplicity because nothing touches the track except the car itself. As the car passes over the track electronic impulses are generated to a computer in the car. The computer analyses the information and provides a numerical print out of the actual condition of the track as well as a profile of each rail. The car logs more than 50,000 miles of track each year. CN has also constructed two additional cars, one for the Canadian Pacific Railway and the other for the Quebec, North Shore and Labrador Railway.

WATER TEMPERATURE DEVICE

This development provides diesel engines with greatly increased protection against temperature control problems. This device utilizes mechanically protected termistors and electronic circuitry to activate various control relays. This major advancement in one of the critical operating areas of diesel locomotive engines was introduced by a CN research team in 1970. This device has now saved many dollars with the reduction of locomotive overheating problems.

PEAK HORSEPOWER METER

This electrical meter, in the form of a digital counter, registers the horsepower rating of diesel locomotives while they are in service. Previously tests of this nature could only be performed in railway maintenance and repair shops, which required locomotives to be removed from service.

LOCOMOTIVE AND TRAIN SIMULATOR

During 1975 Canada's first simulator designed exclusively for the training of locomotive engineers became fully operational. This simulator was developed in a joint effort between the research and operating department staffs, and was built by Canadian National. It simulates actual train operations and complete with sound, visual and motion effects, and provides instantaneous and continuous displays of force levels that occur during train operations. The use of advanced computer technology makes the simulator the most advanced in the world. It is used at CN's locomotive engineer training centre at Gimli, Manitoba, but there are plans for additional installations in other parts of Canada.

The simulator is a direct result of CN's work in the scientific examination of track/train dynamics. It is most ideal for training new top quality locomotive engineers, and it can be used for training personnel in the proper observance of rules and regulations.

IMPROVEMENT OF THE AUTOMATIC CAR IDENTIFICATION SYSTEM (ACI)

All North American railroads have completed or nearly completed the labelling of rolling stock and are currently involved with the installation of trackside scanners, in advance of the implementation of a continent-wide automatic car identification system. In connection with this project, the CN research team developed a computerized system which can be integrated with the standard ACI scanner to provide fast, accurate and more meaningful data on train and car movements. This system eliminates duplicate and repeated material produced by the conventional ACI scanner printer arrangement.

In the normal movement of cars in a yard, individual cars will pass the scanners numerous times in both directions. Rather than producing a cumbersome list of car numbers containing a large percentage of duplication and repetitive information, CN's computerized system monitors the movement from start to finish and continually cancels the excess "ins" and "outs" for the same car. The computer summarizes the entire movement, obtains a record of the net movement, and provides a "clean" list of all cars handled in a particular switching movement.

The computer then compares the clean list with the advance train consist and produces a train list that is virtually 100% valid.

Small digital computers are ideally suited to control small localized segments of the ACI operation, and send to the larger central computer only the information required to control movements on a system basis.

POSITIVE TRACTION CONTROL

One of the latest and most interesting technological advances introduced by CN's research team is an electronic traction correction control unit, which boosts locomotive performance by more than 20%.

THE AUTOMATIC CAR Identification system uses electronic eyes to read striped ACI labels on the sides of the equipment. This system is recording a Temagami-Hamilton unit ore train.
Canadian National

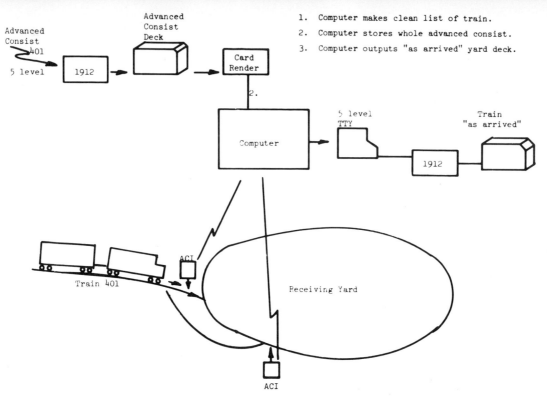

Advanced
Consist
401

5 level

1912

Advanced
Consist
Deck

Card
Render

1. Computer makes clean list of train.
2. Computer stores whole advanced consist.
3. Computer outputs "as arrived" yard deck.

2.

Computer

5 level
TTY

1912

Train
"as arrived"

Train 401

ACI

Receiving Yard

ACI

THIS DIAGRAM DEMONSTRATES the link up between the ACI equipment and the computer.

Canadian National

PTC detects wheel slippage on locomotives and reduces electronically the power being applied to the traction motors. This reduction in power eliminates wheel slippage without affecting the pulling power of the locomotive. Plans are to equip all new locomotives with this device as they are constructed.

BRAKING STUDY

Over the past few years a substantial amount of CN's research work has been in the contract research field. One of these projects was a freight train braking study undertaken in 1972 for the U.S. based Association of American Railroads. The research is expected to result in advanced braking systems for the longer and heavier freight trains of today.

The study utilizes computer simulation techniques as a basis to gather and evaluate data on train action forces during braking. The project was carried out over three year-long phases being completed in late 1975. The results are to be made available to the entire railroad industry.

PASSENGER CAR RIDE

One of the latest projects is the computer based study on the ride, comfort and stability charac-

teristics of a new generation of high speed passenger trains.

This new 120 mph train, designated LRC for lightweight, rapid, comfortable, is being developed by a three member Canadian consortium and is being tested, under contract, by CN's technical research department.

The test procedures were originally developed by the centre to evaluate and improve the degree of comfort on CN's high speed "Rapido," "Tempo" and Turbo passenger trains.

This testing program has brought about improvements to the suspension, banking and safety features of the LRC prototype coach and the tracking characteristics of the high speed diesel locomotives.

Members of the consortium building the LRC are Alcan, MLW Worthington and Dominion Foundries and Steel (Dofasco).

TRAIN HANDLING RECORDER

A train handling recorder has been under the development at the Research Centre since 1971. Designed as a research tool, the recorder gathers information on train operational performance and reproduces the data on magnetic tapes. The recorder operates automatically once train speed reaches two miles per hour. The magnetic tape

174

PART OF Research & Development's job is the evaluation of new passenger equipment. The LRC is now part of the program at the test center. CN is evaluating the LRC under a contract with the builders.

MLW Photo

records 14 hours of actual train operation. The cycle then repeats with the oldest data being erased and new record placed on the tape. The unit records the following types of events:

1. Locomotive speed
2. Locomotive brake cylinder pressure
3. Train line pressure
4. Longitudinal shock
5. Locomotive truck rotation
6. Time of day
7. Engine throttle position
8. Dynamic brake
9. Distance indication
10. Emergency brake applied from cab or train
11. Wheelslip
12. Position of selector handle
13. Sanding
14. Forward or reverse

MECHANIZED TROWELLING

In 1973 CN's research team tackled the most labor intensive part of "trowelling"—a railway term used to describe the removal of ballast from track beds.

By modifying a standard track maintenance machine, CN succeeded in eliminating the manual work associated with the digging out and replacement of ballast at the ends of ties. A Kershaw Ballast Regulator was equipped with two blades, one to plow out the ballast and the other for filling it in. Several modifications were made to the machine's ballast box and hydraulic system. Each machine equals the production of a six member work team.

SUMMARY

These are only a few of the many projects conducted by Research and Development. CN is now earning royalties on many inventions that have been designed, constructed and tested and subsequently sold for manufacture. Railways all over the world now come to the CN for aid and assistance on various types of problems. No other railway in North America has a Research and Development Department as fully equipped as Canadian National's.

The primary source for this chapter came from the Research and Development Department's Handbook describing the Technical Research Centre in Montreal.

In addition to these major non-rail operations, CN operated a number of trucking subsidiaries, international consulting, real estate and Provincial Tankers Limited. The latter operates oil tankers on the Great Lakes.

In conclusion what does this all mean? It means that Canadian National Railways is Canada—one could not exist without the other. The economy of Canada and Canadian National are intertwined with one another, and that is the way it should be. Canada would not be the great nation she is today without CN and her other railways. North Americans and people the world over have much to be thankful for the work and service of Canadian National Railways.

THE MARK OF a good transportation system is the degree in which coordination with other modes of transport is carried out. This photo of a container train in Eastern Canada demonstrates CN's ability in transportation coordination. The containers have arrived by ship, but the major part of their land voyage is by rail although they will reach their final destination by highway.

Canadian National

APPENDIX
CONSOLIDATED ROSTERS

The following steam, diesel, passenger and freight equipment have been designed to assist model railroaders and rail fans with the basic numbering systems of CN equipment. They are not all time rosters for two reasons. Both the steam and diesel rosters in complete form have been published previously. To include all time rosters here would be a duplication of those publications. Further all time rosters would require much more space than is available with this book, since the primary focus is on the operating history of CN service.

The freight and passenger equipment roster concentrate on the rolling stock in service for the last ten to fifteen years. In both cases, complete and detailed studies would require volumns much larger than this one, and would be virtually nothing more than page after page of statistical data.

It is strongly recommended that the reader secure copies of the following publications for a more detailed and complete study of Canadian National, Grand Trunk, Grand Trunk Western, Duluth, Winnipeg & Pacific and Central Vermont steam and diesel power: extra 2200 South issues No. 48, 49 and 50, P.O. Box 41417, Cincinnati, Ohio 45241.

STEAM POWER

Class	Number Series	Wheel Arrangement
A-1 to A-15	100 to 172	4-4-0
B-1 to B-26	212 to 399	4-4-0
C-1 to C-8	400 to 428	2-6-0
D-1 to D-11	470 to 504	2-6-0
E-1 to E-12	530 to 929	2-6-0
F-1 to F-4	1000 to 1015	4-6-0
G-1 to G-21	1016 to 1178	4-6-0
H-1 to H-11	1200 to 1454	4-6-0
I-1 to I-8	1500 to 1628	4-6-0
J-1 to J-7	5000 to 5304	4-6-2
K-1 to K-4	5500 to 5634	4-6-2
K-5	5700 to 5704	4-6-4
L-5 to L-6	1800 to 1804	2-8-0
M-4 to M-5	1805 to 2200	2-8-0
N-1 to N-5	2334 to 2819	2-8-0
O-2 to O-20	7000 to 7543	0-6-0
P-1 to P-5	8000 to 8448	0-8-0
R-1	3000	2-8-2
S-1 to S-4	3198 to 4097	2-8-2
T-1 to T-4	4000 to 4732	2-10-2
U-1	6000 to 6079	4-8-2
U-2 to U-4	6100 to 6410	4-8-4
X-4	10 to 27	4-4-0
X-5	28 to 35	4-6-0
X-6 to X-7	36 to 40	0-4-OT
X-8 to X-9	41 to 44	4-4-2T
X-10	45 to 50	4-6-4T

Newfoundland Narrow Gauge

Class	Number Series	Wheel Arrangement
F-3	15 to 18	4-6-0
L-7	280	2-8-0
R-2	300 to 329	2-8-2
J-8	590 to 599	4-6-2

Source: Canadian National Steam Power

Canadian National Steam Power
By Anthony Clegg and Ray Corley
Copyright 1969
Railfare Enterprises Limited
Box 1434, Station B
Montreal, Quebec

Car Numbers	Type	Inside Dimensions			Doors		Capacity	
		Length	Width	Height	Width	Height	Cu. Ft.	Tons
550000-550034	Box—Steel—International Service	50'6"	9'2"	10'6"	8'0"	9'10"	4866	62
551000-551476	Box—Steel (Stgd. Sliding Doors)	50'6"	9'2"	10'6"	15'1"	9'9"	4860	60
555000-556498	Box—Steel (8' Sliding-8' Plug Doors)	50'6"	9'2"	10'6"	16'0"	9'8"	4860	60-77
559000-559005	Box—Steel (Stgd. Sliding Doors)	50'6"	9'2"	11'0"	15'1"	10'9"	5090	77
426000-429999	Box—Steel Frame	40'6"	8'6"	8'7"	6'0"	8'1"	2990	60
450013-450239	Box—Steel Frame	40'6"	8'6"	8'7"	6'0"	8'1"	2990	60
451000-451099	Box—Steel Frame	40'6"	9'2"	10'1"	6'0"	9'5"	3770	60
461007-464991	Box—Steel Frame	40'6"	8'6"	9'0"	6'0"	8'7"	3098	45
491000-491133	Box—Steel Frame (Equipped)	40'6"	8'6"	8'7"	6'0"	8'1"	2990	61
492000-492003	Box—Steel Frame (Equipped)	40'6"	8'6"	9'0"	6'0"	8'7"	3098	60
500000-514483	Box—Steel Frame	40'6"	8'6"	8'6"	6'0"	8'1"	2990	60
515000-515092	Box—Steel Frame	40'6"	8'6"	9'0"	6'0"	8'7"	3098	45
516000-516242	Box—Steel Frame (1)	36'0"	8'6"	8'0"	5'0"-6'0"	7'7"	2448	47
517051	Box—Steel Frame (Equipped)	40'6"	8'6"	8'7"	6'0"	8'1"	2990	60

(1) Cars 516001 to 516011; 516019 to 516036, 516113, and 516143 to 516180 have 5'0" wide doors.

wood chip car

These cars were specially built, or modified from standard cars, to provide the high cube required for wood chips. Another specialized car for a specialized transportation need.

Car Numbers	Type	Inside Dimensions			Doors		Capacity	
		Length	Width	Height	Width	Height	Cu. Ft.	Tons
850000-850018	Roofless Box—Steel Frame	40'6"	8'6"	11'5"	6'8"	8'6"	3958	60
851000-853046	Roofless Box—Steel Frame	40'6"	8'6"	10'0"-11'3"	13'6"	9'6"	3872	45
854100-855379	Roofless Box—Steel Frame	40'6"	8'6"	11'5"	6'0"	8'1"	3958	60
856000-857076	Roofless Box—Steel	40'6"	9'2"	11'8"	—	—	4325	47
860000-861030	Hopper—Steel	40'8"	10'4"	—	—	—	4488	64-85
871000-871043	Gondola—Steel—Drop Bottom	39'6"	9'8"	9'5"	—	—	3600	82
873000-873148	Gondola—Steel—One top hinged end door	52'6"	9'6"	10'11"	—	—	5445	75
880000-880724	Wood Chip—one top hinged end door	61'5"	9'10"	10'11"	—	—	6600	80
881500-881598	Wood Chip—one top hinged end door	60'3"	10'0"	10'5"	—	—	6300	77

refrigerator cars

Car Numbers	Type	Inside Dimensions			Doors		Capacity	
		Length	Width	Height	Width	Height	Cu. Ft.	Tons
207224-209415	Refrigerator (End Bunker)	35'2''	8'5''	6'7''	5'0''	6'4''	2000	35-37
210006-219012	Refrigerator (Overhd. Ice Tanks)	40'0''	8'5''	6'7''	5'0''	6'8''	2273	35-60
220110-220208	Reefer—Mech. (Fresh Produce)	40'0''	8'6''	7'3''	8'0''	7'3''	2465	55-57
222026-222990	Reefer—Mech. (Fresh Produce) (4)	40'0''	8'6''	6'8''	8'0''	6'7''	2230	55
223000-223062	Reefer—Mech. (Fresh Produce) (2)	40'0''	8'6''	6'8''	8'0''	6'6''	2440	55
224000-225950	Reefer—Mech. (Fresh Produce) (5)	40'0''	8'6''	6'8''	5'0''	6'5''	2273	57

(2) Equipped with compartmentizers.   (4) Equipped with cushioned meat rails.   (5) Equipped with standard meat rails.

Car Numbers	Type	Inside Dimensions			Doors		Capacity	
231000-231074	Reefer—Mechanical (All Purpose)	45'7''	8'8''	8'5''	8'0''	8'8''	3305	70
231103-231171	Reefer—Mechanical (All Purpose)	44'0''	8'8''	9'0''	8'0''	9'0''	3461	67
232000-232001	Reefer—Mech. (All Purpose) (2)	45'7''	8'8''	8'5''	8'0''	8'8''	3305	70
232100-232124	Reefer—Mech. (All Purpose) (2)	44'0''	8'8''	9'0''	8'0''	9'3''	3624	65
233000-233049	Reefer—Mech. (All Purpose) (3)	44'0''	8'8''	8'7''	8'0''	8'7''	3294	67
235000-235299	Reefer—Mech. (All Purpose) (3)	44'0''	8'7''	8'8''	10'6''	8'10''	3270	70

(2) Equipped with compartmentizers.   (3) Equipped with meat rails and trolleys.

insulated box car

Car Numbers	Type	Inside Dimensions			Doors		Capacity	
		Length	Width	Height	Width	Height	Cu. Ft.	Tons
240011-240181	Insulated Box (Converted)	40'0''	8'6''	7'0''	4'11''	6'4''	2380	37
250003-257758	Insulated Box (Converted)	40'0''	8'5''	6'7''	5'0''	6'8''	2264	35-52
280000-280799	Insulated Box	50'6''	8'9''	9'5''	8'0''-9'0''	9'0''	4208	77
283000-284004	Insulated Box (Compartmentizer)	50'6''	8'9''	9'6''	8'0''	9'0''	4208	72-75
286000-286549	Insulated Box (Twin Steel Bulkhead)	50'7''	8'9''	10'2''	10'0''	9'9''	4525	72
289300-289739	Insulated Box (Express Service)	50'6''	8'9''	9'5''	8'0''-9'0''	9'0''	4208	77
290001-290500	Insulated Box	39'7''	8'9''	9'6''	8'0''	9'0''	3300	60-62
290501-290702	Insulated Box	40'6''	8'9''	9'6''	8'0''	9'0''	3380	60
291001-291098	Insulated Box (Compartmentizer)	39'7''	8'9''	9'6''	8'0''	9'0''	3300	60
291099-291346	Insulated Box (Compartmentizer)	40'6''	8'9''	9'6''	8'0''	9'0''	3380	57
291549-291741	Insulated Box	40'6''	8'9''	9'6''	8'0''	9'0''	3300	59
293000-293002	Insulated Box (End Door)	40'6''	8'9''	9'6''	8'0''	9'0''	3380	60

Car Numbers	Type	Inside Dimensions			Capacity	
		Length	Width	Height	Cu. Ft.	Tons
123100-123234	Gondola (Standard)	36'8''	9'6''	5'2''	1750	60
123300-123604	Gondola (Standard)	41'6''	9'6''	5'3''	1998	57-60
136000-138399	Gondola (Standard)	52'6''	9'6''	3'11''	1964	100
140006-140499	Gondola (Standard)	48'6''	9'5''	4'3''	1960	75
141001-142745	Gondola (Standard)	48'6''	9'6''	3'0''	1382	82
143000-143499	Gondola (Standard)	52'6''	9'6''	3'6''	1746	82
143507-150223	Gondola (Standard)	52'6''	9'6''	4'0''	1996	80-82
155000-155199	Gondola (Standard)	65'6''	7'9''	3'6''	1776	75
156000-156399	Gondola (Standard)	65'6''	9'7''	5'0''	3155	92
157000-157299	Gondola (Standard)	65'6''	9'7''	5'0''	3155	92
160000-163105	Gondola (Standard)	48'6''	9'6''	2'9''-4'3''	1300-1960	42-92
191000-191025	Gondola (Standard)	48'6''	9'6''	3'0''	1882	82
192003-192008	Gondola (Standard)	39'9''	8'5''	3'6''	1000	62
193000-193100	Gondola (Container)	52'6''	9'6''	3'6''	1746	82
194000-194004	Gondola (Equipped)	48'6''	9'6''	5'9''	2625	70
194850-194999	Gondola (Standard)	48'6''	9'6''	2'9''	1305	77
98107-99744	Gondola-Hart	40'0''	8'7''	3'6''	1215	55-57
102000-103304	Gondola-Hart (Side Dump)	40'0''	8'7''	3'6''	1215	55-60
104000-105304	Gondola-Hart (Centre & Side Dump)	40'0''	8'7''	3'6''	1215	55-60
123000-123099	Gondola (Side Dump)	36'8''	9'6''	5'2''	1750	60
123235-123299	Gondola (Side Dump)	36'8''	9'6''	5'2''	1750	60
124753-127347	Gondola (Drop Bottom—Side Dump)	36'8''	9'6''	5'2''	1750	60
127728-127856	Gondola (Steel Underframe)	39'10''	8'5''	3'6''-5'0''	1177-1677	47
128000-128975	Gondola (Drop Bottom—Side Dump)	41'6''	9'6''	5'2''	1900-1998	57-60
129000-129182	Gondola (Drop Bottom—Side Dump)	39'6''	9'7''	6'11''	2670	82
130000-130031	Gondola (Coal)	36'8''	9'6''	5'2''	1750	60
131009-132477	Gondola (Drop Bottom—Side Dump)	41'6''	9'6''	5'2''	1900-1998	57-60
132504-132747	Gondola (Drop Bottom—Side Dump)	39'6''	9'7''	6'11''	2670	82
195000-195369	Gondola (Ore)	48'6''	9'6''	2'9''	1300	75-77
196000-196007	Gondola (Drop Bottom Steel Roof)	39'6''	9'7''	6'11''	2670	80
197000-197019	Gondola (Hot Billets)	52'6''	9'6''	4'0''	1906	70
198000-198131	Gondola (Drop Bottom—Side Dump)	31'2''	9'3''	5'3''	1465	82
198200-198404	Gondola (Drop Bottom—Side Dump)	22'11''	9'8''	6'5''	1400	85
198500-198649	Gondola (Ore)	35'1''	8'6''	7'0''	2300	105
198700-198742	Gondola (Drop Bottom—Side Dump)	25'11''	9'8''	5'4''	1300	84
199000-199199	Gondola (Coal)	54'4''	9'8''	8'4''	3900	102

livestock cars

Car Numbers	Type	Inside Dimensions			Doors		Capacity	
		Length	Width	Height	Width	Height	Cu. Ft.	Tons
170147-173730	Stock	36'0''	8'6''	8'0''	6'0''	7'7''	2448	32-47
800000-801207	Stock	36'0''	8'6''	8'0''	6'0''	7'7''	2448	32-47
802000-802091	Stock (Feed Racks)	36'0''	8'6''	8'0''	5'0''	7'6''	2467	32-47
810000-810638	Stock (1)	40'6''	8'6''	8'7''	6'0''	8'1''	2990	45
810639-810704	Stock	40'6''	9'0''	9'0''	6'0''	8'6''	3265	42
810706-810733	Stock	40'6''	8'6''	9'0''	6'0''	8'6''	3098	45
810734-810972	Stock	40'6''	8'6''	10'0''	6'0''	9'6''	3442	45
830001	Horse (16 Stalls)	47'8''	9'0''	6'11''	4'5''	7'0''	2967	40

(1) Cars 810126; 810300 to 810499 equipped with adjustable louvers for ventilation.

| 815000-815174 | Stock—Double Deck | 40'6'' | 8'6'' | {5'3'' / 5'6''} | 6'0'' | {4'11'' / 5'6''} | 3585 | 57 |

automobile cars

Car Numbers	Type	Inside Dimensions		Capacity in Tons
		Length	Width	
700000-700404	Automobile (Tri-Level)	89'1''	8'2''	45
700500-700649	Automobile (Tri-Level)	89'4''	8'4''	45
702000-702417	Automobile (Tri-Level)	89'1''	8'3''	40-43
710000-710404	Automobile (Bi-Level)	89'1''	8'2''	45
710500-710649	Automobile (Bi-Level)	89'4''	8'3''	48
711000-711079	Automobile (Bi-Level)	87'4''	8'2''	48
711080-711090	Automobile (Bi-Level)	89'4''	8'4''	48
711100-711109	Automobile (Bi-Level)	85'0''	8'2''	47
711110-711111	Automobile (Bi-Level)	89'1''	8'2''	52
711112-711119	Automobile (Bi-Level)	85'0''	8'2''	47
711121-711126	Automobile (Bi-Level)	85'0''	8'2''	47
750000-750211	Automobile Flat—Pedestal	89'4''	8'3''	48

Car Numbers	Type	Inside Dimensions			Doors		Capacity	
		Length	Width	Height	Width	Height	Cu. Ft.	Tons
589006-589473	Automobile (End Doors)	40'6''	9'2''	10'6''	15'0''	9'8''	3898	45
720000-720069	Double Deck Auto Transporter	56'5''	8'10''	{5'9'' / 5'10''}	9'0''	{5'10'' / 5'10''}	—	32
730000-730073	Double Deck Auto Transporter	74'5''	8'10''	{5'9'' / 5'10''}	9'0''	{5'10'' / 5'10''}	—	25-40
740000-740361	Auto (Staggered Side & End Doors)	40'6''	9'2''	10'6''	15'0''	9'8''	3898	45
794000-794004	Automobile (1)	50'6''	9'2''	10'11''	9'0''	10'4''	5082	75
796000-796223	Automobile (1)	50'6''	9'2''	10'6''	15'1''	9'9''	4860	55
797000-797014	Automobile (1)	50'6''	9'2''	10'11''	9'0''	10'4''	5082	70
799000-799015	Automobile (1)—International Service	60'9''	9'2''	10'9''	16'0''	10'9''	5880	60-80

(1) Equipped to handle Automobile Parts.

flat

Car Numbers	Type	Inside Dimensions			Capacity in Tons
		Length	Width	Height	
600002-600074	Flat (Bulkhead)	49'0''	9'4''	8'6''	57-60
601000-601014	Flat (Bulkhead) (1)	48'8''	9'4''	8'6''	75-80
602001-603024	Flat (Bulkhead) 14 Chain Tie-Downs	49'0''	9'4''	10'6''	60-72
606000-609199	Flat (Bulkhead) 12 Chain Tie-Downs and Stakes	51'6''	9'4''	10'9''	75-82
610000-610364	Flat (Bulkhead) in Aluminum Ingot Service	51'0''	9'2''	4'3''	77-80
611000-611049	Flat (Bulkhead) 6 Chain Tie-Downs and Stakes (2)	51'6''	9'4''	10'9''	80
611062-611111	Flat (Bulkhead) 6 Chain Tie-Downs and Stakes (1)	51'11''	9'4''	9'6''	75
611200-611299	Flat (Bulkhead) 12 Chain Tie-Downs	51'6''	9'4''	10'7''	79
612001-612104	Flat (Bulkhead) 6 Chain Tie-Downs and Stakes	51'5''	9'3''	9'6''	57
613000-613351	Flat (Bulkhead) 12 Chain Tie-Downs and Stakes (2)	51'6''	9'4''	10'9''	77
614050-614129	Flat (Bulkhead) 12 Chain Tie-Downs and Stakes	51'5''	9'2''	9'6''	57
615000-615249	Flat (Bulkhead) 12 Chain Tie-Downs and Stakes (2)	51'6''	9'4''	10'9''	80
615250-615999	Flat (Bulkhead) (2)	51'5''	9'4''	10'8''	75-80
617000-617069	Flat (Bulkhead) (2)	51'6''	9'4''	10'10''	80
619000-619049	Flat (Inclined Bulkhead) (2)	49'1''	9'4''	10'9''	77
630000	Flat (Container)	46'1''	9'0''	—	35
631001-631040	Flat (Container)	40'0''	8'8''	—	30
632000	Flat (Container)	46'1''	9'0''	—	65
633000-633199	Flat (Container)	60'3''	8'8''	—	30
633500-633508	Flat (Container) Equipped	60'3''	8'8''	—	30
634000-634054	Flat (Container) I.S.O.	46'1''	9'0''	—	47
634100-634731	Flat (Container) I.S.O.	{40'0''- 41'0''}	8'8''	—	47
635000-635494	Flat (Container)	80'5''	8'8''	—	78-80
639000-639137	Flat (Container)	46'1''	8'8''	—	47
639501-639626	Flat (Container)	80'5''	8'8''	—	101
640000-640142	Flat (Bulkhead) Pulpwood	30'5''	9'4''	9'7''	50-65
650000-650004	Flat—Steel	35'8''	9'0''	—	52
651499-653759	Flat—Steel	41'7''	9'0''	—	50
654002-654034	Flat—Steel	46'0''	8'10''	—	62-65
657079	Flat—Steel (1)	52'6''	10'4''	—	77
659001-659993	Flat—Steel	40'5''	9'0''	—	65
660000-660009	Flat—Steel	61'0''	9'1''	—	45
661004-662689	Flat—Steel	52'0''	9'5''	—	60
662690-663454	Flat—Steel	52'6''	10'2''	—	57
663600-664100	Flat—Steel	52'6''	10'4''	—	62
664900-664924	Flat—Steel—6 Chain Tie-Downs	52'0''	9'5''	—	60
665001-665499	Flat—Steel (2)	53'6''	9'4''	—	85
665500-665590	Flat—Steel (2)	52'6''	9'2''	—	77-82
666000-666449	Flat—Steel	54'4''	9'4''	—	82
667000-667099	Flat—Steel (2)	60'11''	9'2''	—	100
670000	Flat (Centre Well) Well—18'1'' by 6'0'' (2)	36'9''	10'0''	—	80
672000-672009	Flat (Depressed) Depression—21'0'' long —2'4'' above top of rail (2)	59'9''	8'10''	—	135
673000-673001	Flat (Depressed) Depression—25'0'' long—2'4'' above top of rail (2)	63'9''	8'10''	—	137
674000-674003	Flat (Depressed) Depression—25'0'' long—2'4½'' above top of rail (2)	66'11''	7'9''	—	167
675000-675001	Flat (Depressed) Depression—25'0'' long—2'5½'' above top of rail (2)	52'8''	9'0''	—	180
680100-689174	Piggyback Flat Cars	—	—	—	—
690007-690105	Flat—Steel (Log Service)	52'0''	9'3''	10'2''	57-60
691000-691047	Flat—Steel (Steel Rod Service)	40'5''	8'10''	5'6''	65
693000-693125	Flat—Steel (Log Service)	52'0''	8'11''	7'8''	60
694000-694046	Reel Car	53'6''	10'4''	—	80
695000-695004	Flat—Equipped	89'1''	8'2''	—	57
696000-696022	Flat—Steel—International Service	85'0''	8'2''	—	70
699000-699023	Flat (Container)	—	—	—	50-65
751000-751524	Flat—Steel—Auto Parts	53'6''	9'4''	—	60-80
752000-752036	Flat—Steel—Auto Parts—International Service	56'1''	10'6''	—	70

(1) Loads over 118,000 pounds must be equally distributed over car.

(2) See Equipment Register re distribution of load.

container cars

Car Numbers	Type	Inside Dimensions		Capacity in Tons
		Length	Width	
631001-631040	Container Flat (Express)	40'0''	8'8''	30
633000-633199	Container Flat (Express)	60'3''	8'8''	30
633500-633508	Container Flat (Equipped)	60'3''	8'8''	30
634000-634054	Container Flat (I.S.O. Containers)	46'1''	9'0''	45
634100-634731	Container Flat (I.S.O. Containers)	40'0''	8'8''	45
635000-635494	Container Flat (I.S.O. Containers)	80'5''	8'8''	78-80
639000-639137	Container Flat (I.S.O. Containers)	46'1''	8'8''	47
639501-639526	Container Flat (I.S.O. Containers)	80'5''	8'8''	101

Newfoundland

Car Numbers	Type	Inside Dimensions			Doors		Capacity	
		Length	Width	Height	Width	Height	Cu. Ft.	Pounds
2601 to 2829	Flat, Steel Frame	40'0''	8'6''	—	—	—	—	75,000
2851 to 2949	Flat, Steel Frame	40'0''	8'6''	—	—	—	—	75,000
6200 to 6213	Insulated Cars	35'2''	7'9''	6'11''	6'10''	6'8''	1970	50,000
6275 to 6284	Box, Steel, Heated, Note 74	40'0''	8'6''	7'10''	5'0''	6'9''	2660	75,000
6300 to 6313	Box, Steel, Heated, Note 32	39'7''	8'9''	9'6''	8'0''	9'0''	3300	85,000
6400 to 6449	Ballast, Steel	37'0''	8'6''	4'7''	—	—	—	60,000
6755 to 6799	Hopper, Steel	36'0''	8'6''	—	—	—	1490	100,000
6807 to 6881	Gond. Steel, Fixed Sides & Ends, Drop Bot.	36'0''	8'6''	4'0''	—	—	1224	100,000
7000 to 7024	Stock	35'10''	8'2''	7'4''	6'0''	7'0''	2180	70,000
7025 to 7039	Stock	35'10''	8'2''	7'4''	6'0''	6'11''	2180	70,000
7100 to 7104	Mechanical Refrig. Steel, Notes 19, 131 see exception	43'10''	8'5''	8'4''	8'0''	7'6''	3050	70,000
7101	Mechanical Refrig. Steel, Notes 19,131	43'10''	8'5''	7'5''	8'0''	7'6''	2735	70,000
7150 to 7159	Mechanical Refrig., Notes 5, 19	40'0''	8'6''	6'8''	8'0''	6'7''	2273	75,000
7275 to 7429	Refrig. Basket Bunkers, Steel Frame, Notes 1, 2	29'5''	7'9''	6'4''	5'0''	6'8''	1445	50,000
7560 to 7584	Box, Steel Frame, Note 79	36'0''	8'2''	7'5''	7'6''	7'0''	2200	70,000
7585 to 7659	" " "	36'0''	8'2''	7'5''	7'6''	7'0''	2200	65,000
7660 to 7848	" " "	36'0''	8'2''	7'5''	7'6''	7'0''	2200	70,000
7849 to 7908	" " "	35'10''	8'2''	7'5''	7'6''	7'0''	2181	70,000
7909 to 7998	" " "	35'10''	8'2''	7'5''	7'6''	7'0''	2181	70,000
7999 to 8098	" " "	35'10''	8'2''	7'5''	7'6''	6'11''	2199	70,000
8099 to 8348	" " "	35'10''	8'2''	7'5''	7'6''	6'11''	2199	70,000
8400 to 8509	Box, Steel	40'6''	9'2''	10'0''	6'0''	9'5''	3712	95,000
8900 to 9076	Box, Steel Frame	35'10''	8'2''	7'5''	11'7''	6'11''	2199	70,000
10900 to 10909	Auto, Steel Frame, Note 20	36'0''	8'2''	7'5''	7'6''	7'0''	2200	65,000
10910 to 10934	Auto, Steel Frame, Note 20	40'0''	8'2''	7'5''	7'6''	7'0''	2432	65,000
11766 to 11795	Flat, Steel Frame	40'0''	8'6''	—	—	—	—	75,000
11796 to 11842	Flat, Steel Frame	32'6''	8'3''	—	—	—	—	75,000
11843 to 12015	Flat, Steel Frame	40'0''	8'6''	—	—	—	—	75,000
12016 to 12365	Flat, Steel Frame	40'0''	8'8''	—	—	—	—	75,000
13000 to 13129	Flat	40'0''	8'8''	—	—	—	—	110,000
13500 to 13599	Pulpwood, Flat, Rack End	33'6''	8'8''	9'0''	—	—	—	105,000
13630 to 13649	Pulpwood, Flat, Rack End	35'6''	8'8''	9'0''	—	—	—	105,000
14000 to 14246	Pulpwood, Flat, Rack End	33'6''	8'6''	8'0''	—	—	—	70,000
14290, 14291	Flat, Depressed Center, Steel Frame	40'0''	8'6''	—	—	—	—	80,000
14292, 14293	Flat, Depressed	46'9''	9'0''	—	—	—	—	120,000
16000 to 16024	Flat, Container	42'0''	8'8''	—	—	—	—	70,000
16025 to 16027	Flat, Container	40'0''	8'6''	—	—	—	—	70,000
16030 to 16033	Flat, Container	46'1''	9'0''	—	—	—	—	65,000
16040 to 16045	Flat, Container	52'0''	9'5''	—	—	—	—	50,000
16300 to 16339	Flat, Container	46'1''	9'0''	—	—	—	—	50,000
18000 to 18019	Flat, Bi-Level Loader	55'0''	8'6''	—	—	—	—	55,000

Grand Trunk Western Railroad Company

Car Numbers	Type	Inside Dimensions			Doors		Capacity	
		Length	Width	Height	Width	Height	Cu. Ft.	Tons
206150-206394	Refrigerator, Steel Underframe	30'8''	8'7''	7'4''	5'0''	6'4''	1883	37
206400-206499	Refrigerator, Steel	40'0''	8'6''	6'10''	5'0''	6'9''	2295	55
206900-206999	Refrigerator, Steel Underframe	35'0''	8'4''	6'7''	5'0''	6'4''	1920	37
302000-302026	Refrigerator, Steel, Cushion Underframe	50'1''	9'3''	9'6''	10'0''	9'3''	4598	67
302027-302029	Refrigerator, Steel, Cushion Underframe	49'9''	8'10''	9'4''	10'0''	9'1''	4131	70
302030-302032	Refrigerator, Steel, Cushion Underframe	50'1''	9'5''	9'11''	10'0''	9'3''	4578	70
302033-302062	Refrigerator, Steel, Underframe	50'1''	9'5''	9'11''	10'0''	9'3''	4604	70
106500-108499	Coal, Steel, Double Hopper	30'0''	9'6''	—	—	—	1735	55
111600-112199	Coal, Steel, Triple Hopper	40'7''	10'4''	—	—	—	2608	77
113700-113874	Covered Hopper, Steel	29'3''	9'6''	—	—	—	1958	77
113875-113974	Covered Hopper, Steel	41'1''	9'6''	—	—	—	2893	77
136000-136049	Covered Hopper, Steel	46'0''	9'11''	—	—	—	4000	77
138000-138049	Covered Hopper, Steel, 2 pocket	29'3''	9'11''	—	—	—	2600	102
138050-138074	Covered Hopper, Steel, 3 pocket	53'3''	10'5''	—	—	—	4600	95
145000-145399	Gondola, Steel, Fixed Ends Wood Floor (1)	50'0''	10'0''	4'0''	—	—	2000	70-77
145400-145699	Gondola, Steel, Fixed Ends, Wood Floor (1)	53'1''	9'5''	3'6''	—	—	1749	77
145700-146299	Gondola, Steel, Fixed Ends, Wood Floor (1)	50'6''	9'10''	4'0''	—	—	1986	70-77
180000-180024	Stock, Steel Frame, Double Deck	40'0''	8'6''	9'0''	6'0''	4'1''	2912	42
182025-182039	Stock, Steel Frame, Single Deck	40'6''	9'2''	10'0''	12'0''	9'6''	3712	42
303000-303011	Flat, Steel, Truck Saddleback Ldg.	89'4''	8'4''	—	—	—	—	72
303100-303122	Flat, Steel, Flush Deck, Cushioned Underframe	89'0''	9'0''	—	—	—	—	67
303123-303156	Flat	89'2''	9'0''	—	—	—	—	72
303200-303258	Flat	89'0''	8'2''	—	—	—	—	55-90
303300-303393	Flat (Flushdeck)	89'4''	10'2''	—	—	—	—	75
303500-303772	Flat, Low Deck	89'0''	8'2''	—	—	—	—	55-65
304000-304054	Flat, Bi-Level Auto Racks	89'4''	8'4''	6'10''	—	—	—	51
304200-304238	Flat, Low Deck	89'1''	8'2''	—	—	—	—	55
304500-304926	Flat, Tri-Level Auto Racks	89'0''	8'2''	—	—	—	—	55-90
305000-305999	Auto, Steel, Cushioned Underframe, Plug Doors	60'10''	9'4''	10'9''	16'0''	10'8''	6091	70-100
306000-306917	Auto, Steel, Cushioned Underframe, Plug Doors, Auto Parts	86'6''	9'4''	12'9''	10'-20'	11'0''-12'9''	5727-10000	70-100
307000-307049	Flat, Steel, Cushion Underframe	48'0''	7'4''	—	—	—	—	99
307050-307149	Flat, Coil Steel	48'0''	7'4''	—	—	—	—	100
308000-308099	Auto, Steel, Cushion Underframe	40'6''	9'2''	10'6''	10'0''	9'9''	3898	55
309000-309299	" " " "	50'6''	9'6''	10'7''	10'0''	10'0''	4893	70
309400-309434	" " " "	49'5''	9'3''	10'6''	10'0''	9'8''	4500	75
309500-309502	" " " "	44'3''	9'2''	11'2''	16'0''	10'9''	4510	94
315000-315024	Covered Hopper, Steel	49'9''	10'7''	—	—	—	4650	100
315050-315099	Covered Hopper, Steel (2)	34'9''	10'7''	—	—	—	2970	100
315100-315129	Covered Hopper	54'7''	10'1''	—	—	—	4740	97
316000-316014	Covered Hopper, Steel	29'6''	9'11''	11'9''	—	—	2600	50
317000-317011	Covered Hopper, Steel, Airslide	29'6''	9'11''	—	—	—	2600	50
375000-375058	Auto, Steel, Equipped	60'9''	9'2''	10'9''	16'0''	10'9''	6013	75
375060-375324	Auto, Steel, Cushioned Underframe, Equipped	60'9''	9'3''	10'9''	16'1''	10'9''	6040	70
376000-376012	Auto, Steel, Equipped, Cushioned Underframe	60'9''	9'4''	11'6''	10'0''	11'0''	6347	87

Car Numbers	Type	Inside Dimensions			Doors		Capacity	
		Length	Width	Height	Width	Height	Cu. Ft.	Tons
378000-378251	Auto, Steel, Equipped, Plug Doors Cushioned Underframe	86'6''	9'2''	12'9''	20'0''	12'9''	10000	40
383000-383575	Auto, Steel, Equipped, Cushioned Underframe	60'9''	9'4''	11'6''	10'0''	11'0''	6347	65-87
385000-385010	Auto, Steel, Equipped	60'9''	9'4''	11'6''	16'0''	11'0''	6615	65-82
385011-385018	Auto, Steel, Equipped, Cushioned Underframe	60'9''	9'3''	10'9''	16'1''	10'9''	6040	62
441500-441849	Box, Steel, Equipped	40'6''	9'2''	10'6''	8'0''	9'10''	3898	42-44
454000-454021	Wood Chip, Steel, Triple Hopper	40'3''	9'4''	—	—	—	4467	70
460000-460599	Box, Steel, Some Equipped	40'6''	8'9''	9'4''	6'0''	8'9''	3312	42
470250-470749	Box, Steel, Some with Roof Hatches	40'6''	9'2''	10'4''	6'0''	9'9''	3835	40-45
515000-516599	Box, Steel, some with 14'6'' doors and some Equipped	40'6''	9'2''	10'6''	7'0''	9'10''	3898	55-60
516600-516899	Box, Steel, some Equipped	40'6''	9'2''	10'5''	8'0''	9'10''	3882	55-62
572700-572999	Box, Steel Frame	40'6''	8'6''	10'0''	6'0''	9'8''	3443	45
573000-573099	Box, Steel	50'6''	9'2''	10'6''	8'4''	9'10''	4861	44
575000-575999	Box, Steel Frame, Staggered Doors, some Equipped, some with 6' Doors	40'6''	8'6''	10'0''	12'0''	9'7''	3443	44
581000-581999	Box, Steel Frame	40'6''	8'6''	9'0''	6'0''	8'7''	3098	44
583200-583701	Box, Steel Frame, Staggered Doors and End Doors	40'6''	9'2''	10'0''	10'6''	9'6''	3712	42
585203-585884	Box, Steel, End Doors	40'6''	9'2''	10'6''	13'6''	9'10''	3898	44
586500-587923	Box, Steel Frame, Staggered Doors, some Equipped	40'6''	9'2''	10'4''	12'0''	9'6''	3835	44
591000-591199	Box, Steel, Staggered Doors and End Doors	50'6''	9'2''	10'4''	14'6''	9'8''	4785	44
591200-591599	Box, Steel, Staggered Doors and End Doors (1)	50'6''	9'2''	10'6''	16'6''	9'10''	4861	44-52
591600-591799	Box, Steel, Staggered Doors and End Doors	50'6''	9'2''	10'4''	14'6''	9'8''	4785	40-44
592000-595499	Box, Steel, some Equipped	50'6''	9'2''	10'6''	8'4''	9'10''	4861	32-44
595500-596049	Box, Steel, some Equipped	50'6''	9'2''	10'6''	8'0''	9'10''	4866	45-57
596050-596449	Box, Steel, some Equipped	50'6''	9'2''	10'5''	15'6''	9'11''	4840	37-57
596500-596699	Box, Steel, Equipped	50'6''	9'4''	10'5''	15'4''	9'10''	4853	55
599500-599942	Auto, Steel, some with Cushioned Underframe, Equipped	50'6''	9'4''	10'6''	15'0''	9'10''	4952	52-77
599943-599992	Box, Steel, Cushioned Underframe, some Equipped	50'6''	9'4''	10'6''	10'0''	9'10''	4932	77
616400-616874	Flat, Steel, some Equipped, some with Bulkheads	53'6''	9'5''	—	—	—	—	70-77
619000-619509	Flat, Steel, some Equipped	60'0''	10'6''	—	—	—	—	72-75
670000-670099	Flat, Steel, some Equipped	51'11''	9'4''	—	—	—	—	50-60
675000-675094	Flat, Steel, Cushioned Underframe	47'6''	7'0''	—	—	—	—	97
675095-675099	Flat, Steel, Cushioned Underframe	48'0''	7'0''	—	—	—	—	97

(1) Some of these cars have nailable steel floors.

(2) Car 315052 is a slurry car and may be unloaded by slurry method only.

No	VOLTAGE	AIR COND./CLIMATISATION	TYPE	TYPE
5180-5181 (2 cars/voit.)	32	ICE/GLACE	64-seat Coach	Coach 64 places
5183-5190 (8 cars/voit.)	"	" "	"	" "
5192-5193 (2 cars/voit.)	"	" "	"	" "
5195	"	" "	"	" "
5197-5214 (18 cars/voit.)	"	" "	"	" "
5215	"	" "	"	" "
(Equipped with 2 oil space heaters)equipee de 2 chaufferettes à huile)				
5216	32	ICE/GLACE	64-seat Coach	Coach 64 places
5217	"		48-seat Snack Coach	Coach casse-croûte 48 places
5218	"	" "	64-seat Coach	Coach 64 places
5219-5220 (2 cars/voit.)	"	" "	48-seat Snack Coach	Coach casse-croûte 48 places
5221-5229 (9 cars/voit.)	"	" "	64-seat Coach	Coach 64 places
5236	"	" "	66-seat Coach	Coach 66 places
5241	"	" "	"	"
5283-5291 (9 cars/voit.)	"	" "	64-seat Coach	Coach 64 places
5293-5299 (7 cars/voit.)	"	" "	"	"
5301-5307 (7 cars/voit.)	"	" "	"	"
5375	"	NAC/NÉANT	Commuter Coach	Coach banlieue
5382-5383 (2 cars/voit.)	"	ICE/GLACE	60-seat Coach	Coach 60 places
5386	"	" "	"	"
5388-5390 (3 cars/voit.)	"	" "	"	"
5393-5395 (3 cars/voit.)	"	" "	"	"
5399-5400 (2 cars.voit.)	"	" "	"	"
5402-5403 (2 cars/voit.)	"	" "	"	"
5405-5407 (3 cars/voit.)	"	" "	"	"
5409	"	" "	"	"
5411-5419 (9 cars/voit.)	"	" "	"	"
5421-5436 (16 cars/voit.)	"	" "	"	"
5437	114	EM	Coach	Coach
5439-5444 (6 cars/voit.)	"	"	"	"
5446-5449 (4 cars/voit.)	"	"	"	"
5452	"	"	"	"
5454-5456 (3 cars/voit.)	"	"	"	"
5458-5459 (2 cars/voit.)	"	"	"	"
5464-5465 (2 cars/voit.)	"	"	"	"
5467-5474 (8 cars/voit.)	"	"	"	"
5476	"	"	"	"
5478	"	"	"	"
5481-5483 (3 cars/voit.)	"	"	"	"

No	VOLTAGE	AIR COND./CLIMATISATION	TYPE	TYPE
5485-5492 (8 cars/voit.)	114	EM	Coach	Coach
5494-5495 (2 cars/voit.)	"	"	"	"
5497-5501 (5 cars/voit.)	"	"	"	"
5503-5506 (4 cars/voit.)	"	"	"	"
5508-5509 (2 cars/voit.)	"	"	"	"
5511-5512 (2 cars/voit.)	"	"	"	"
5514	"	"	"	"
5516-5519 (4 cars/voit.)	"	"	"	"
5522	"	"	"	"
5525	"	"	"	"
5527	"	"	"	"
5529-5534 (6 cars/voit.)	"	"	"	"
5536-5537 (2 cars/voit.)	"	"	"	"
5541-5542 (2 cars/voit.)	"	"	"	"
5544	"	"	Snack Coach	Coach casse-croûte
5545	"	"	Coach (crew room)	Coach (chambre réservée au personnel)
5547-5548 (2 cars/ 2 voit.)	"	"	" " "	Coach (chambre réservée au personnel)
5552	"	"	Snack Coach	Coach casse-croûte
5558	"	"	Coach	Coach
5560	"	"	Snack Coach	Coach casse-croûte
5562	"	"	Coach	Coach
5569	"	"	"	"
5571	"	"	"	"
5573	"	"	Snack Coach	Coach casse-croûte
5574	"	"	Coach	Coach
5576	"	"	"	"
5578-5591 (14 cars/voit.)	"	"	"	"
5593-5597 (5 cars/voit.)	"	"	"	"
5598	"	"	Snack Coach	Coach casse-croûte
5599	"	"	Coach	Coach
5602-5603 (2 cars/voit.)	"	"	"	"
5610-5611 (2 cars/voit.)	"	"	"	"
5616-5618 (3 cars/voit.)	"	"	"	"
5619	"	"	Buffeteria Coach Lge	Coach buffet-bar
5620	"	"	Snack Coach	Coach casse-croûte
5621-5622 (2 cars/voit.)	"	"	Coach	Coach
5623	"	"	Coach (crew room)	Coach (chambre réservée au personnel)
5624	"	"	Coach	Coach

No	VOLTAGE	AIR COND./ CLIMATISATION	TYPE	TYPE
5625	114	EM	Buffeteria Coach Lounge	Coach buffet-bar
5626-5628 (3 cars/voit.)	"	"	Coach	Coach
5629-5630 (2 cars/voit.)	"	"	Snack Coach	Coach casse-croûte
5631-5634 (4 cars/voit.)	"	"	Coach	Coach
5635	"	"	Snack Coach	Coach casse-croûte
5636-5638 (3 cars/voit.)	"	"	Coach	Coach
5640-5644 (5 cars/voit.)	"	"	"	"
5645	"	"	Snack Coach	Coach casse-croûte
5646-5654 (9 cars/voit.)	"	"	Coach	Coach

NOTE:

Snack coaches (EM) have 72 seats.

Buffeteria coach lounges (EM) have 36 coach seats and 24 lounge seats.

Coaches (EM) equipped with crew room have 72 seats.

The following are (EM) 76-seat coaches equipped with ski racks:

REMARQUES:

Les coachs casse-croûte (EM) ont 72 places.

Les coachs buffet-bar (EM) ont 36 places coach et 24 places lounge.

Les coachs (EM) équipés d'une chambre reservée au personnel ont 72 places.

Les numéros suivants sont des coachs (EM) de 76 places equipés de supports à skis:

5469	5508	5562
5470	5519	5597
5494	5527	5627

Coahces (EM) equipped with seat trays are:

Les coachs (EM) suivants sont équipés de plateaux à la place:

5602	5618	5626	5637	5642	5647	5651
5603	5621	5628	5638	5643	5648	5652
5616	5622	5631	5640	5644	5649	5653
5617	5624	5636	5641	5646	5650	5654

Coaches (EM) NOT equipped with storage lockers are:

Les coachs (EM) suivants NE SONT PAS équipés d'armoire de stockage:

5440	5456	5467	5505	5525	5537	5578	5583	5603	5636
5441	5458	5471	5509	5529	5548	5579	5586	5617	5638
5449	5464	5489	5511	5531	5558	5581	5591	5622	5644
5455	5465	5491	5522	5533	5576	5582	5599	5624	5649

No	VOLTAGE	AIR COND./ CLIMATISATION	TYPE	TYPE
5700	114	EM	Dayniter	Coach Super-confort
5701	"	"	"	" " "
5702	"	"	"	" " "
5703	"	"	"	" " "
5704	"	"	"	" " "
5705	"	"	"	" " "
5706	"	"	"	" " "
5707	"	"	"	" " "
5708	"	"	"	" " "
5709	"	"	"	" " "
5710	"	"	"	" " "
5711	"	"	"	" " "
5712	"	"	"	" " "
5713	"	"	"	" " "
5714	"	"	"	" " "
5715	"	"	"	" " "
5716	"	"	"	" " "
5717	"	"	"	" " "
5718	"	"	"	" " "
5719	"	"	"	" " "
5720	"	"	"	" " "
5721	"	"	"	" " "
5722	"	"	"	" " "
5723	"	"	"	" " "
5724	"	"	"	" " "
5725	"	"	"	" " "
5800	32	NAC/NEANT	Commuter Coach	Coach banlieue
5802-5803 (2 cars/voit.)	"	" "	"	"
5805	"	" "	"	"

RAILINERS/AUTORAILS

6000-6002 (3 cars/voit.)	64	EM	Coach	Coach
6003	"	"	Coach (snack)	Coach (casse-croûte)
6004-6006 (3 cars/voit.)	"	"	Coach	Coach
6100-6101 (2 cars/voit.)	"	"	"	"
6102	"	"	Coach (snack)	Coach (casse-croûte)
6104-6106 (3 cars/voit.)	"	"	Coach	Coach
6107	"	"	Coach (snack)	Coach (casse-croûte)
6108	"	"	Coach	Coach
6109	"	"	Coach (snack)	Coach (casse-croûte)

No	VOLTAGE	AIR COND./ CLIMATISATION	TYPE	TYPE
6110-6111 (2 cars/voit.)	64	EM	Coach	Coach
6112	"	"	Coach (snack)	Coach (casse-croûte)
6113-6114 (2 cars/voit.)	"	"	Coach	Coach
6115	"	"	Coach (snack)	Coach (casse-croûte)
6116	"	"	Coach	Coach
6117	"	"	Coach (snack)	Coach (casse-croûte)
6118	"	"	"	"
6200	"	"	Coach & Baggage (snack counter)	Coach-fourgon à bagages (casse-croûte)
6201	"	"	Coach & Baggage	Coach-fourgon à bagages
6202-6203 (2 cars/voit.)	"	"	Coach & Baggage (snack counter)	Coach-fourgon à bagages (casse-croûte)
6204	"	"	Coach & Baggage	Coach-fourgon à bagages
6205	"	"	Coach & Baggage (snack counter)	Coach-fourgon à bagages (casse-croûte)
6206	"	"	Coach & Baggage (snack counter)	Coach-fourgon à bagages (casse-croûte)
6207	"	"	Coach & Baggage	Coach-fourgon à bagages
6208	"	"	"	" "
6209	"	"	"	" "
6210	"	"	"	" "
6302	"	"	"	" "
6350-6356 (7 cars/voit.)	"	"	"	" "
6401	"	NAC/NÉANT	Baggage	Fourgon à bagages
6450	"	"	"	"
6453	"	" "	"	" "
6475	"	" "	"	" "

COMMUTER COACHES/COACHS BANLIEUE

No	VOLTAGE	AIR COND./ CLIMATISATION	TYPE	TYPE
6602-6604 (3 cars/voit.)	32	NAC/NÉANT	Commuter Coach	Coach banlieue
6606	"	"	"	"
6608-6609 (2 cars/voit.)	"	" "	"	"
6730-6735 (6 cars/voit.)	64	" "	"	"
6739-6749 (11 cars/voit.)	"	" "	"	"
7169	32	" "	Passenger & Baggage	Voyageurs & bagages
7186	"	" "	"	"
7188	"	" "	"	"
7197	"	" "	"	"
7201	"	" "	"	"

No	VOLTAGE	AIR COND./ CLIMATISATION	TYPE	TYPE
7207	32	NAC/NÉANT	Passenger & Baggage	Voyageurs & bagages
7209-7210 (2 cars/voit.)	"	"	"	"
7360	"	" "	"	"
9200-9202 (3 cars/voit.)	"	" "	Baggage Cars	Fourgons à bagages
9209	"	" "	Baggage-Dormitory	Fourgons-dortoirs
9211	"	" "	"	"
9218-9221 (4 cars/voit.)	"	" "	Baggage Cars	Fourgons à bagages
9228-9237 (10 cars/voit.)	"	" "	"	"
9239-9244 (6 cars/voit.)	"	" "	"	"
9246-9260 (15 cars/voit.)	"	" "	"	"
9262-9269 (8 cars/voit.)	"	" "	"	"
9278-9302 (25 cars/voit.)	"	" "	"	"
9475-9488 (14 cars/voit.)	64	EM	Baggage-Crew	Fourgons-dortoirs
9500-9507 (8 cars/voit.)			Auto-Transporter	Wagon porte-autos
15204-15205 (2 cars/voit.)			Battery Charging Car	Chargeur (accumulateurs)
15300-15302 (3 cars/voit.)(Tempo)			Electric Generator Unit	Générateur électrique

(Battery

SOURCE:

Office of:
Manager, Equipment Development & Control,
H.Q. Passenger Sales and Services,
Montreal, Quebec,
1 January, 1974

Bureau du Directeur,
Parc de matériels voyageurs, Contrôle et Développement,
Direction générale, Ventes et Services voyageurs,
Montréal, Québec,
le 1er janvier 1974.

INDEX